Revise
KS3
English

Kath Jordan

Contents

English at Key Stage 3

Introduction to English at KS3

This book is designed for you to use at home to support your study at school. The topics covered in each chapter meet the requirements of the **National Curriculum for English** at Key Stage 3.

The National Curriculum separates English into three Attainment Targets.

Attainment Target 1 – Speaking and Listening

Throughout Key Stage 3 you will learn and develop skills that will enable you to communicate more effectively. You will learn to speak confidently and fluently in a range of formal and informal situations. You will also explore a range of roles in group work including: contributing to, supporting and managing discussion. You will improve your listening skills and your ability to interpret tone of voice and gestures.

Attainment Target 2 – Reading

During your KS3 studies you will have the opportunity to read and respond to a range of texts: **plays, novels, poetry, non-fiction** and **media**. You will read modern **texts and writing from other historical periods**, including plays by **Shakespeare**. The skills you will develop are: **reading for meaning, understanding and responding to texts** and **understanding the author's craft**. You will have the opportunity to practise different reading techniques for different purposes.

Attainment Target 3 – Writing

Through your reading you will identify a range of techniques used to create particular effects in writing. You will learn to manage these techniques to make your own writing more effective. The major writing styles you will develop are: writing to **imagine, explore, entertain**; writing to **inform, explain, describe**; writing to **analyse** and **comment**; and writing to **persuade** or **argue**. You will also learn to **plan, draft** and **present** your work to make the most of the skills you have learned.

The Framework for Secondary English

The **Framework for Secondary English at Key Stage 3** identifies each of the key skills and requirements of the National Curriculum. You will find information about Framework objectives in the margin throughout most chapters of this book.

Word and Sentence level

In each chapter you will find **Word level** and/or **Sentence level** panels. These panels will give you advice about: **specific spelling rules, vocabulary choices, sentence grammar** and **Standard English**. This information is usually related to the main content of the page or pages you have been studying and is intended to support your text level study.

Text Level

You will notice that the reading and writing chapters in this book often use the same texts. This will help you to identify particular techniques and then try them out in your own writing.

How this book will help

National Curriculum Levels

There is information about how to achieve each **National Curriculum Level (4–7)** at the beginning of each **chapter**. This information will help you to identify the skills you need to improve and develop. Most students aim to achieve **Level 5 or 6** by the end of **Key Stage 3**.

Speaking, Listening, Reading and Writing

The book is separated into four main sections. The first three cover the Attainment Targets: **Speaking and Listening, Reading and Writing**. Each section will help you to learn, develop and revise the important skills in each area.

The Reading and Writing chapters aim to provide range, development and extension to cover the whole of Key Stage 3. The **Shakespeare** topic in **Chapter 2** will be particularly helpful if your school uses the Year 9 Optional Tests on Shakespeare.

The final section covers **spelling**, **punctuation** and **grammar**. Here you will find strategies to improve your **spelling** and a helpful reference guide to enable you to refine your **punctuation** and make conscious decisions about the **grammatical structures** you use.

Assessment

The final level you are awarded at the end of Key Stage 3 may be the product of a range of assessments. Your school may use the **Optional Tests** for Years 7, 8 and 9 or they may have their own end-of-year tests. Your school may also use **APP (Assessing Pupil Progress)**. APP allows you and your teacher to assess your progress for each **Assessment Focus (AF)** in Speaking and Listening, Reading and Writing. This may be done by assessing your ongoing class work or through a specifically set assessment question. Your work may be assessed against one or more AFs. There are four AFs for Speaking and Listening, seven AFs for Reading and eight AFs for Writing.

You will find an explanation of what each Assessment Focus is about on page 157 of this book. Your teacher will use APP grids which set out what you should be able to do to achieve a particular level in each AF.

Questions

Each chapter has a range of questions and tasks that will help you to test your level of understanding and refine your skills, as well as preparing you for **Optional Tests** in Years 7, 8 and 9 and APP tasks.

This book will help you to **check your progress and understanding** in three ways:
- **Progress Check tests**
- **Have a go tasks**
- **Assessment questions**

Checking your progress

Progress Checks

At the end of each **topic** in the **Speaking and Listening**, **Reading** and **Writing** sections you will find a short **Progress Check** test that covers the key points in that topic. Each question usually requires a true or false, multiple choice or one-word answer. The answers are printed upside down at the bottom of the test panel. Use these tests immediately after completing a topic to ensure that you understand the main points.

Have a go tests

In the **Speaking and Listening** and **Writing** sections you will find slightly longer **Have a go** tasks which extend the examples given in the topic you have studied. This is your chance to practise the new skills you have learned.

Assessment questions

You will find questions at the end of each chapter, which will be useful for your revision for Optional Tests and formal examinations or preparation for APP tasks. The examples will give you the chance to practise a range of question and task styles you might expect to encounter during Key Stage 3. Each of the reading questions tests your skill in a particular Assessment Focus. The writing tasks allow you to test whichever Assessment Focus you feel needs most improvement.

Some answers and general guidance can be found at the back of the book on pages 148–152.

Preparing for assessment

How to revise in English

In English your revision should focus on practising skills rather than learning facts. Follow these steps for successful revision.

Step 1

Identify the skills that you have weaknesses in.
Ask your class teacher to help you with this where necessary.
Prioritise your revision topics and make a revision timetable or diary.

Step 2

Study the topic to be learned.
Work through the examples.
Annotate the texts you are working on and make notes.
Learn key terms and techniques.

Step 3

Attempt practice questions.
Focus on the skills identified in the topic you have studied.
Make sure you allow the correct amount of time for each question.

Step 4

Compare your answers to the examples in the topic you have studied.
Identify areas of weakness that need further development.

Step 5

Review your notes, annotations and exam answers for each topic regularly.

Good luck!

1 Speaking and listening

After studying this section you should be able to:

- talk and listen with confidence in a range of contexts
- take on different roles in group discussions
- understand how drama can help with your English studies

To achieve the following National Curriculum levels, across a range of contexts, you need to do the following for each level.

Level 4
- Speak in **extended** turns to **express ideas and feelings** with **relevant detail**.
- **Structure** talk to support meaning.
- Take on straightforward **roles** and **responsibilities** in pairs and groups.
- Vary **vocabulary**, **grammar** and **non-verbal features** to suit **audience** and **purpose**.

Level 5
- **Explain** ideas and feelings and make **meaning explicit**.
- **Shape talk** in deliberate ways to **engage** the listener, including **adapting** vocabulary, grammar and non-verbal features.
- **Sustain** roles and responsibilities with **independence** in pairs and groups.

Level 6
- **Explore complex** ideas and feelings in a range of ways.
- **Organise talk** to guide the listener and demonstrate **empathy** and **understanding** through flexible choices of vocabulary, grammar and non-verbal features.
- Adopt a **range** of roles and responsibilities in group talk and **promote effective discussion**.

Level 7
- Explore a **wide range** of subject matter with **precision** and **effect**.
- **Manage** and **manipulate** talk through apt choice of vocabulary, grammar and non-verbal features.
- **Sustain** effective collaboration and discussion in a range of group roles and responsibilities.

1.1 Speaking and listening

Speaking and listening is not tested in any formal examinations at Key Stage 3. However, it is a very important element of your studies. Your English teacher will decide on the levels you receive for speaking and listening and this assessment will form part of your final **Teacher Assessment level** at the end of Key Stage 3.

Some of the activities you take part in will be quite **formal** and **assessed** in an obvious way; however, at other times your teacher will be making **informal judgements** about your speaking and listening work without you even realising it. For this reason, it is important that you **make the most of all of your speaking and listening opportunities**.

Tasks you might expect

You might expect to carry out the following tasks:
- **asking questions** in class
- **answering questions** in class
- **giving a talk** (formal or informal)
- **reading aloud**.

Asking questions

This is an excellent way to **improve your levels of understanding**. Asking a question does not always mean that you don't understand what your teacher is talking about. Even if you do understand everything, you should still ask questions. It allows you to look beneath the surface for less obvious meanings. You will be given credit for asking intelligent and searching questions.

Answering questions

You should always attempt to answer questions in group discussions or oral tests. Even if you get the answer wrong, **you will be given credit for thinking and trying your best**. If you don't feel sure of an answer you should still have a go. You may have approached the problem from another angle or thought of something that your teacher did not consider. It does happen!

Reading aloud

This is a skill that can only be developed with practice. Always speak clearly and stand or sit up straight. **Read according to the punctuation to maintain the sense of what you are reading**. Think about the content of the piece you are reading and try to express the emotions of the characters you are reading by varying the pace and tone of your voice.

Giving a persuasive talk

In Chapter 8 you will learn about writing a persuasive speech or talk. However, writing the speech is only half the skill – the way you present it is just as important.

The speech printed on page 10 is an extract from a speech about climate change and the importance of wind energy in combating climate change.

Key Point	In order for a speech to be effective, in addition to being well written it must be delivered in a persuasive and powerful way.

As you read the speech, think about how you would deliver it. How would you give emphasis to the important parts of the speech?

Some of the key words and phrases have been highlighted for you.

So I ask **you all**:
Do **you** want to put a **stop** to climate change?
Do **you** want to use **clean**, **renewable** energy that won't harm our precious environment? Do **you** want to save the **future** of our planet?

If the answer to these questions is **yes**, then – please – join us in our campaign for the development of wind energy.

Wind farms have the potential to provide **us – and our future generations –** with an energy source that is natural; an energy source that is clean; an energy source that will **not** run out.

Wind farms can be placed on farmland and farmers are still able to farm around them or alternatively they can be built offshore, where there's plenty of wind and where they aren't even visible from land! And **most importantly**, once built, wind farms can provide a clean, renewable source of energy. They **do not** leave behind **harmful** pollution or **hazardous** waste products.

An eyesore, some will say.
But what about coal mines – **filthy blots** on the landscape. What about oil rigs – **ugly and dangerous**.
Consider the disaster with the oil leak in the Gulf of Mexico. Consider the **damage** it has done to the ocean, its inhabitants, the coast and the scenery. **It is a disgrace!** But whilst fossil fuels continue to be used as our main energy source, it is, unfortunately, only too likely to happen again. **This simply cannot be allowed!**

If we are to save our environment, **we must act now**.
We must act to support a **future** that is clean; a **future** that is renewable; a **future** of wind energy!

How to give emphasis to your speech

AF4
You should be able to identify the main methods used by presenters to explain, persuade, amuse or argue a case.

- **Vary the pace** – this speech begins with a series of rhetorical questions to grab the audience's attention and get them to agree with the speaker. This technique lends itself to the speaker speeding up slightly towards the climax of the final question, thereby enabling the speaker to build up tension in the speech.
- **Think about the rhythm** – the repetition in this speech of certain words (e.g. *future*, *clean*), and particularly of sentence structure, helps to create a powerful rhythm.

AF1
You should be able to make a **formal presentation** in **standard English**, using appropriate rhetorical devices.

- **Tone of voice** – think about how to deliver each section of the speech.
- **Emphasis** – think about particular words and phrases that may require more emphasis.
- **Gestures** – think about ways in which you could give more emphasis to your words through your hand gestures and facial expressions. Remember, open gestures, such as showing your palms, suggest honesty; clenched fists suggest power; and closed gestures such as folded arms suggest defence or dishonesty.

Progress Check

Have a go

1. Read this speech out loud, experimenting with the way you give emphasis to different parts of the speech.
2. If you write your own speech after working through the tasks in Chapter 8, practise delivering it in a persuasive way. Ask friends or family to be your audience.

1.2 Group discussion

Tasks you might expect

AF2
You should be able to recognise and build on other people's contributions.

You might expect to carry out the following tasks:
- **informal paired discussion**
- **informal group discussion**
- **formal debate**.

Informal discussion

You will often be asked to discuss work in small groups (not just in English). The subject might be a poem, a character's strengths and weaknesses, a new approach to a problem or a social issue. The key to success is to **speak and listen**. This will allow you to share information and develop new ideas before presenting them to a larger group. You will lose marks if you remain silent and just listen. You will also lose marks if you are aggressive or you talk too much and ignore the ideas of others.

Key Point

If you are not confident in speaking and listening, then try to note down at least one point or question and make sure you use it in the debate or discussion.

Formal debate

There are rules and procedures to follow in a debate, which your teacher will explain to you. The important thing to remember is that you must use

Standard English. Do not use slang, colloquialism or dialect words. A debate is about listening to others as well as putting your own point across. You will develop a much stronger argument if you listen and respond to the points made by the opposition. **Make sure that you listen to their points and respond to them, as well as putting forward your arguments**.

Key Point	If you are confident about speaking in a group, then help others by asking supportive questions to bring in a weaker member of your group or by reinforcing a point made by somebody else.

Roles in group discussions

You will be given the opportunity to take on a **range of roles** when you take part in group work. Read through the guidelines below and try to apply them in your group work at school.

Key Point	In group work you will be asked to **lead**, **contribute** or **support**. In a formal debate the roles are more clearly defined: **chairperson**, **proposer** and **seconder**, **opposer** and **seconder**.

AF2
You should be able to adopt a **range of roles** in discussion, including acting as spokesperson, and contribute in different ways.

Leading

If you are leading the group you will need to:
- **organise** the group
- **plan** how to complete the task
- keep other students **on task**
- **summarise** the main points made by others
- **identify differences** of opinion and help to **resolve** them
- **change the direction** of the discussion or refocus the task.

Contributing

If you are a contributor to the discussion, you will need to:
- **introduce** new ideas
- **express your opinion** and **respond** to the opinions of others
- **share** ideas and information
- **listen attentively**.

Supporting

If you are asked to support others, you will still have the opportunity to contribute as above, but you should also:

- **ask others specific questions**, in order to bring them into the discussion
- **encourage others** to contribute
- **build on the ideas of others**, reinforcing their points.

Sentence level

There are many differences between speaking and writing. The key points that typify speech are:

- we rely on **tone, pace, facial expression and gestures** to get meaning across – in writing we have to rely on punctuation to do this
- speech is usually **spontaneous**, whereas writing is often planned
- we don't always speak in full sentences and speech can be interrupted
- vocabulary is often more **informal**, especially in conversation
- we use **non-standard forms** when talking informally
- sentence structure is much looser because speech often includes 'fillers', e.g. *you know*, *sort of*, *like* and hesitations, e.g. *er. . .*, *um. . . .*

1.3 Drama

At your school you may study drama as part of your English lessons, or you may have separate drama lessons as part of your timetable. However drama is organised at your school, you will probably find that your English teacher uses some drama techniques with you as part of your English studies. You may even use drama techniques such as **hot seating** and **improvised role-play** in other school subjects.

Why is drama important?

Not everybody enjoys acting and performing, but even if you don't want to be an actor in the future, drama is very important.

Drama helps you to develop many important life skills:

- **working as a team**
- **communicating clearly**
- **problem solving**
- **developing trust**.

Drama can also help you with your studies in English. It helps you to:

- **empathise** with characters
- **explore** the inner thoughts, feelings and motivations of characters in fiction
- **understand** the techniques used by Shakespeare and other playwrights you might study.

Drama techniques you might use

Key Point	The term **in character** means that you should speak, behave and react as the character you are playing, **not** as yourself. A **stimulus** is a piece of information, such as a picture, a prop or a few lines of dialogue to use as a starting point for a piece of drama.

Hot seating

With this technique one person sits in the 'hot seat', **in character**. The rest of the group, who are not in character, take it in turns to ask the character in the hot seat questions about their decisions, motivation, thoughts about what has happened in the scene and so on. The person in the hot seat must answer in character.

This technique can be very helpful in **exploring the inner thoughts and feelings of a character** in a novel or play you are studying in English lessons.

Thought tracking

This is another useful technique for exploring the inner thoughts and feelings of a character.

You may be given the command to **freeze** during work on a **scripted** or **improvised** scene. If you are spotlighted or tapped on the shoulder, you should speak out loud the thoughts and feelings of your character at that point in the scene.

Tableaux

A **tableau** is a still picture or image, also known as a **freeze frame**. It could be a key moment in a scene, frozen in time. This is useful because it gives the audience more time to take in what is happening. You can use **tableaux** to illustrate emotions, ideas and relationships. This technique is also useful for creating definite beginnings and endings for pieces of drama.

> ### Word level
>
> Many words in the English language are borrowed from other languages: **tableau** is French. Tableau forms its plural by adding an **x**. Other French words commonly used in English follow the same rule: tableau → tableaux, gateau → gateaux, bureau → bureaux.

Improvisation

When you **improvise** you make up a scene **without** working from a script. Improvisation can be **spontaneous** or **rehearsed**. Spontaneous improvisation is made up on the spot in response to a given **stimulus**. The scene is performed without rehearsal or preparation. In rehearsed improvisation, you are given time to prepare and practise, making alterations and improvements as you go.

Script work

When you work with a script you should respond to the stage directions. Think carefully about the character you are playing and what you want to do with the basic information you have about that person. Think about the way you want your character to move and speak, and what they look like. Try to find one or two props that help you to identify with the character you are playing.

Key Point

- A prop (property) is an object used to enhance a piece of drama – to make it more realistic or identify a particular character.
- Stage directions are used in a script to give actors instructions about where to move, how to say particular lines and when to come on and off stage.

Progress Check

Have a go

1. Make sure you get the chance to practise each of the group talk roles in your class work.
2. Plan a talk on a subject you are interested in. Make a tape recording of your talk so you can work out how to improve your performance.
3. Choose a passage from your reading book and practise reading aloud at home.
4. Discuss the news, your homework or recent events in your favourite soap opera with a friend or your family.

2 Reading fiction and plays

After studying this section you should be able to:

- understand characters and their development
- comment on the setting of stories and plays
- understand relationships and their development
- understand the importance of openings
- study the plays of Shakespeare in an informed way

To achieve the following National Curriculum levels you need to do the following for each level.

Level 4
- Recognise what the **characters** are like.
- Have a **general understanding** of the whole text.
- Show an **understanding** of the **plot**.

Level 5
- Begin to read beneath the surface for **meaning**.
- Note the **effect of particular words** and **phrases**.
- Show some **understanding** of the **feelings and behaviour of the characters**.

Level 6
- **Support your ideas** about characters and relationships with **detailed reference to the text**.

- Write in some detail about the writer's **use of language** and the **structure** of the text.
- Comment on the **creation of setting and atmosphere**.
- Give a **personal response** to the text.

Level 7
- Show **understanding** of the more **complex feelings** of the characters.
- Recognise what the writer is trying to achieve and how they do this.
- Trace the **development of plot, character and relationships** and **themes**.
- Give a **personal** and **critical response** to the text.

2.1 Characters

Character descriptions

In order to write convincing descriptions, an author needs to know the characters very well. Authors don't necessarily describe the character in detail – they may drop in clues about personality as the story progresses. J K Rowling, the author of the *Harry Potter* stories, claims to have a complete history for all of her characters in her head.

Appearance

The way a character **looks** gives the reader important clues about what kind of person they might be. **Descriptions** are vital in helping the reader to imagine what the character looks like. Vivid descriptions make characters seem real, even if they are a little unusual! Read the following description of Albus Dumbledore, from *Harry Potter and the Philosopher's Stone*.

> Nothing like this man had ever been seen in Privet Drive. He was tall, thin and very old, judging by the silver of his hair and beard, which were both long enough to tuck into his belt. He was wearing long robes, a purple cloak which swept the ground and high-heeled, buckled boots. His blue eyes were light, bright and sparkling behind half-moon spectacles and his nose was very long and crooked, as though it had been broken at least twice. This man's name was Albus Dumbledore.
>
> From *Harry Potter and the Philosopher's Stone* by J K Rowling

First impressions

The above extract is the first description of the wizard, Albus Dumbledore, in the book. From this description the reader makes some initial judgements about the character – he is:

- **unusual**
- **mysterious**
- **magical**
- **wise**.

Dumbledore is the first wizard character to be introduced in the book, and in this description the fact that he is very different from the inhabitants of Privet Drive is emphasised. His **magical qualities** are also highlighted by the use of words like *silver*, *bright* and *sparkling*.

False impressions

Some descriptions can be **misleading**. Sometimes writers try to create a particular impression of a character so that they can surprise the reader later.

Read the following descriptions of Rubeus Hagrid. What is your first impression of the character?

> If the motorbike was huge, it was nothing to the man sitting astride it. He was almost twice as tall as a normal man and at least five times as wide. He looked simply too big to be allowed, and so wild – long tangles of bushy black hair and beard hid most of his face, he had hands the size of dustbin lids and his feet in their leather boots were like baby dolphins. In his vast, muscular arms he was holding a bundle of blankets.
>
> * * * *
>
> A giant of a man was standing in the doorway. His face was almost completely hidden by a long, shaggy mane of hair and a wild, tangled beard, but you could make out his eyes, glinting like black beetles under all the hair.
>
> From *Harry Potter and the Philosopher's Stone* by J K Rowling

This character seems quite frightening and imposing. This is because the writer has chosen to emphasise two of Hagrid's distinct qualities:

- his size: *twice as tall as a normal man*; *simply too big to be allowed*; *vast* and *giant*
- his connection with animals: *shaggy mane*; *baby dolphins*; *like black beetles*. The word *wild* is also repeated.

There is a clue in the description that Hagrid will not always be frightening. Look again at the final sentence of the second extract. His eyes are described as *glinting*. This word could suggest that there is also a smile lost under his enormous beard.

Hagrid can be very kind and he is always willing to put himself out to protect Harry Potter. There are two sides to his character, and **descriptions of his behaviour and speech help to form a more reliable impression of him.**

Behaviour

Read the extracts below from *Harry Potter and the Philosopher's Stone*.

> Harry looked up into the fierce, wild, shadowy face and saw that the beetle eyes were crinkled in a smile.
>
> * * * *
>
> Hagrid looked at Harry with warmth and respect blazing in his eyes. . .
>
> * * * *
>
> But he had finally gone too far. Hagrid seized his umbrella and whirled it over his head. "NEVER –" he thundered, "– INSULT – ALBUS – DUMBLEDORE – IN – FRONT – OF – ME!"
>
> He brought the umbrella swishing down through the air to point at Dudley – there was a flash of violet light, a sound like a firecracker, a sharp squeal and next second, Dudley was dancing on the spot with his hands clasped over his fat bottom, howling in pain. When he turned his back on them, Harry saw a curly pig's tail poking through a hole in his trousers.

These short extracts show how Hagrid's behaviour can change depending on whom he is dealing with.

Notice how the choice of **verbs** in the final extract indicates Hagrid's anger: *seized*, *whirled*, and *thundered*.

Speech

The way a character speaks can give the reader more **valuable clues** about him or her. As you read the next extract, think about:

- **what Hagrid says**
- **the way he speaks**
- **the way his speech is described**.

> 'Shouldn'ta lost me temper,' he said ruefully, 'but it didn't work anyway. Meant ter turn him into a pig, but I suppose he was so much like a pig anyway there wasn't much left ter do.'
>
> He cast a sideways look at Harry under his bushy eyebrows.
>
> 'Be grateful if yeh didn't mention that ter anyone at Hogwarts,' he said. 'I'm – er – not supposed ter do magic, strictly speakin'. I was allowed to do a bit ter follow yeh an' get yer letters to yeh an' stuff – one o' the reasons I was so keen ter take on the job –'

What he says

This shows that Hagrid isn't a bad person really – he knows he's done wrong, but he couldn't help himself. What he says about Dudley also shows that he is honest and won't stay quiet to spare someone's feelings.

The way he speaks

The way Hagrid's speech is written represents his **accent and dialect**. He doesn't speak in Standard English; his character would seem too formal if his speech was written in that form. Like a description of appearance, **the way a character speaks helps the reader to imagine them as a real person**.

The way his speech is described

Instead of always writing 'he said', the writer uses a range of **verbs** and **adverbs** to describe the way Hagrid speaks. This helps the reader to work out how a character feels when they are speaking:

- *he thundered* (verb) shows us that he is angry
- *he said ruefully* (adverb) shows that he is sorry about what he's done.

Sentence level

A **noun phrase** is a group of words with a noun as the central component. In fiction, the noun phrase is used to make writing more interesting and to add explanatory or descriptive detail. The other components of a noun phrase are usually **adjectives**.

The example below shows how J K Rowling uses a noun phrase to extend the description of Hagrid.

- Harry looked up into the **face** (noun)
- *Harry looked up into the **fierce, wild, shadowy face*** (noun phrase)

Perhaps it had something to do with living in a dark cupboard, but Harry had always been small and skinny for his age. He looked even smaller and skinnier than he really was because all he had to wear were old clothes of Dudley's and Dudley was about four times bigger than he was. Harry had a thin face, knobbly knees, black hair and bright-green eyes. He wore round glasses held together with a lot of Sellotape because of all the times Dudley had punched him on the nose. The only thing Harry liked about his own appearance was a very thin scar on his forehead which was shaped like a bolt of lightning.

From *Harry Potter and the Philosopher's Stone* by J K Rowling

---

Progress Check

Read the extract above, a description of Harry Potter, and answer these questions.

1. How is the reader supposed to feel about Harry?
2. Why are his glasses broken?
3. What details are emphasised most?
4. What is the most unusual thing about Harry's appearance?
5. What is the effect of mentioning the scar last?

1 We are supposed to feel sorry for him. 2 He has been punched by Dudley. 3 His size: he's very small and thin. 4 His lightningbolt scar. 5 This makes it seem important.

2.2 Setting

Describing the setting and creating an atmosphere

Read the extract below from David Almond's novel, *Kit's Wilderness*. It is the first description of a very important setting for the first part of the novel, Askew's den. In this description Almond uses **a range of devices to create atmosphere and give the reader a real sense of the place**.

The words and phrases that are highlighted are what create the atmosphere and provide vivid description in this extract.

Try reading the extract, leaving out the words and phrases that are highlighted.

Without these highlighted words and phrases, there is very little descriptive detail and, as a result, there isn't a real sense of the setting or atmosphere.

In Stoneygate there was a wilderness. It was an empty space between the houses and the river, where the ancient pit had been. That's where we played Askew's game, the game called Death. We used to gather at the school's gates after the bell had rung. We stood there whispering and giggling. After five minutes, Bobby Carr told us it was time and he led us through the wilderness to Askew's den, a deep hole dug into the earth with old doors slung across it as an entrance and a roof. The place was hidden from the school and from the houses of Stoneygate by the slope and by the tall grasses growing around it. The wild dog Jax waited for us there. When Jax began to growl, Askew drew one of the doors aside. He looked out at us, checked the faces, called us down.

    We stumbled one by one down the crumbling steps. We crouched against the walls. The floor was hard-packed clay. Candles burned in niches in the walls. There was a heap of bones in a corner. Askew told us they were human bones, discovered when he'd dug this place. There was a blackened ditch where a fire burned in winter. The den was lined with dried mud. Askew had carved pictures of us all, of animals, of the dogs and cats we owned, of the wild dog, Jax, of imagined monsters and demons, of the gates of Heaven and the snapping jaws of Hell. He wrote into the walls the names of all of us who'd died in there. My friend Allie Keenan sat across the den from me. The blankness in her eyes said: You're on your own down here.

Key Point

The devices used in this piece of writing are:
- descriptive detail
- particular vocabulary choices
- imagery
- sentence structure.

Vocabulary choices

Some of the vocabulary choices the author made are significant:
- *stumbled*, *crouched* – the **verb** choices give the impression that the characters feel nervous and uncertain in this setting
- *ancient*, *empty* – used alongside the word *wilderness*, these **adjectives** add to the impression of an unwelcoming and threatening place.

Descriptive detail

The additional detail that describes the den, its surroundings and the people who go there helps to make the setting seem more realistic.
- **The den** – the candles, the blackened ditch and the heap of 'human' bones give the den a frightening feel.
- **The surroundings** – the fact that the den is hidden from the school and the houses is significant. It reinforces the idea that the game of death is dangerous and probably forbidden. The den is detached from civilisation and this makes it more threatening.
- **Allie Keenan** – the description focuses more on place than people, but the additional detail about Allie is revealing. It suggests that people change their character when they are in the den. The narrator describes Allie as his friend, but in the sentence that follows her behaviour is distinctly unfriendly: *The blankness in her eyes said: You're on your own down here*.

Imagery

Imagery is used sparingly in this extract, but this makes it more effective.
- **Personification** – the author personifies Hell: *the gates of Heaven and the snapping jaws of Hell*. This image connects to the game of death, introduced earlier in the extract. It is intended to remind the characters and the reader of the possibilities that follow death. It also reminds the reader of the snapping jaws of *the wild dog Jax*.

Sentence structure

AF2
The comma in this sentence is a caesura.

A range of sentence structures is used in this extract.
- *That's where we played Askew's game, the game called death*. The structure of this sentence means that information about the subject of the game is delayed. Usually we would connect playing a game with fun. The phrase that follows the comma in this sentence reveals the more sinister nature of this particular game.
- Most of the sentences in the second paragraph are **short, simple sentences**.
- The sentence which begins *Askew had carved. . .* is much **longer** and has a **more complicated structure**, allowing the author to create a different effect.
- *Askew had carved pictures of us all, of animals, of the dogs and cats we owned, of the wild dog, Jax, of imagined monsters and demons, of the gates of Heaven and the snapping jaws of Hell*. This sentence places real domestic creatures alongside imagined demons and the frightening image of Hell. The list form of this sentence helps to **build up tension** as the images become less familiar and more frightening.

2.3 Relationships

We all have relationships – with family, friends, teachers or work colleagues. To be believable, fictional characters must **develop relationships** within a text. The development of a relationship can often be the central element of the plot.

AF7
You should be able to **recognise** how texts refer to and reflect the **culture in which they were produced**.

The extract below is taken from *A Kestrel for a Knave*, a novel written in 1968. This passage deals with the relationship between the main character, Billy Casper, and one of his teachers, Mr Sugden. As you read this extract think about:

- how you would describe the **relationship**
- how the writer **creates tension** between the two characters
- how the writing might **reflect the time in which it was produced**.

He thought this was funny, Billy didn't. So Sugden looked round for a more appreciative audience. But no one was listening. They faced up for a few more seconds, then Billy turned back to his peg. He undressed quickly, bending his pumps free of his heels and sliding them off without untying the laces. When he stood up the black soles of his socks stamped damp imprints on the dry floor, which developed into a haphazard set of footprints when he removed his socks and stepped around pulling his jeans down. His ankles and knees were ingrained with ancient dirt which seemed to belong to the pigmentation of his skin. His left leg sported a mud stripe, and both his knees were encrusted. The surfaces of these mobile crusts were hair-lined, and with every flexion of the knee these lines opened into frown-like furrows.

* * * *

The **exclamation marks** show that Billy is in pain or discomfort.

Notice that the conversation is written as these people would really speak. '**Gi'o'er**' is how Billy would say 'Give over'. Billy doesn't speak in Standard English – this style of writing indicates Billy's dialect and accent.

The whole conversation shows that Mr Sugden is more powerful than Billy.

Mr Sugden's final comment shows that he thinks Billy is a liar.

The conversation isn't always written in complete sentences because we don't always speak in complete sentences.

While he worked on his ankles and heels Sugden stationed three boys at one end of the showers and moved to the other end, where the controls fed into the pipes on the wall. . .The blunt arrow was pointing to HOT. Sugden swung it back over WARM to COLD. For a few seconds there was no visible change in the temperature, and the red slice held steady, still dominating the dial. Then it began to recede, slowly at first, then swiftly, its share of the face diminishing rapidly.

The cold water made Billy gasp. He held out his hands as though testing for rain, then ran for the end. The three guards barred the exit.

'Hey up, shift! Let me out, you rotten dogs!' They held him easily so he swished back to the other end, yelling all the way along. Sugden pushed him in the chest as he clung his way round the corner.

'Got a sweat on, Casper?'

'Let me out, Sir. Let me come.'

'I thought you'd like a cooler after your exertions in goal.'

'I'm frozen!'

'Really?'

'Gi' o'er, Sir! It's not right!'

'And was it right when you let the last goal in?'

'I couldn't help it!'

'Rubbish, lad.'

Billy tried another rush. Sugden repelled it, so he tried the other end again. Every time he tried to escape the three boys bounced him back, stinging him with their snapping towels as he retreated. He tried manoeuvring the nozzles, but whichever way he twisted them the water still found him out. Until finally he gave up, and stood amongst them, tolerating the freezing spray in silence.

When Billy stopped yelling the other boys stopped laughing, and when time passed and no more was heard from him, their conversations began to peter out, and attention gradually focused on the showers. Until only a trio was left shouting into each other's faces, unaware that the volume of noise in the room had dropped. Suddenly they stopped, looked round embarrassed, then looked towards the showers with the rest of the boys.

The cold water had cooled the air, the steam had vanished, and the only sound that came from the showers was the beat of water behind the partition; a mesmeric beat which slowly drew the boys together on the drying area.

The boy guards began to look uneasy, and they looked across to their captain.

'Can we let him out now, Sir?'

'No!'

From *A Kestrel for a Knave* by Barry Hines

How relationships can be depicted

The central feature of the relationship described in the extract from *A Kestrel for a Knave* is the **abuse of power**. In this relationship the teacher has all the power and the pupil has none. The physical bullying that goes on in the extract reflects the kind of behaviour that actually happened in some schools at the time the novel was written.

There are several ways that relationships and their development can be depicted in literature, including the use of:
- **dialogue**
- **character behaviour**
- **other characters.**

Dialogue

You can learn a lot about relationships between characters from **what they say to each other**. The annotations beside the text on page 23 explain many of the key features of the dialogue.
- Mr Sugden's **questions** show that he doesn't believe anything that Billy says.
- Mr Sugden's speech is quite **controlled** because he is in control of the exchange and the situation.
- Billy's **exclamations** show that he is more **emotional** and doesn't have any control over the situation.
- Mr Sugden's tone is **sarcastic**; this reflects his resentment about losing the football match.

Character behaviour

Mr Sugden behaves like a bully. He has all the power in the relationship and he exploits this:
- he thinks Billy's predicament is funny
- he gets the other boys on his side and uses them to punish and humiliate Billy
- he turns the shower to cold
- he pushes and shouts at Billy.

Billy has **no power** and he is unable to change the situation he finds himself in:
- he tries to escape but the other pupils prevent him from doing this
- he gives up and tolerates the freezing spray in silence.

Other characters

- Billy's poor relationship with the other boys makes it easier for Mr Sugden to pick on him.
- The other boys look up to Mr Sugden and are pleased to act as his guards.
- The way that the boys react at the end of the extract shows that even they think he has gone too far.
- The fact that the boys feel sorry for Billy makes the reader feel even more **sympathy** for him.

Word level

Lots of words in this extract end in **-tion**: *pigmentation*, *conversation*, *attention*, *partition*, *exertion*.

There are many different ways to spell the '**shun**' ending sound: -tion, -sion, -ssion, -cian. Use **-tion** when:

- there is a long vowel sound before the 'shun' sound, e.g. **conversation**
- there is a consonant before the 'shun' sound, e.g. **attention**
- there is a short 'i' sound before the 'shun' sound, e.g. **partition**, except words with '**mission**', e.g. **permission**.

Progress Check

1. What gives the first clue that the boys are beginning to worry about Billy?
2. Find three words in the first paragraph that describe the mud and which have a similar meaning.
3. What is the effect of using all three words?

3 It emphasises how dirty Billy is. 2 ingrained, encrusted, crusts 1 The other boys stopped laughing.

2.4 Openings

The opening of a short story or the first chapter of a novel is **crucial**. The author has to get the reader's interest straightaway to convince them to keep on reading. It is important for the writer to get the right **balance** between giving enough information for the reader to decide whether they will enjoy the book, and keeping enough back for a few surprises along the way.

The following extract is a first chapter from a novel. As you read it, think about what makes it an effective opening chapter.

This is what Fliss dreamed the night before Year 7 went to Whitby.

She was walking on a road high above the sea. It was dark. She was alone. Waves were breaking at the foot of cliffs to her left, and further out, the moonlight made a silver path on the water.

In front of her was a house. It was a tall house looming blackly against the sky. There were many windows, all of them dark.

Fliss was afraid. She didn't want to go inside the house. She didn't even want to walk past but she had no control over her feet. They seemed to go by themselves, forcing her on.

She came to a gate. It was made of iron, worked into curly patterns. Near the top was a bit that was supposed to be a bird in flight – a seagull perhaps – but the gate had been painted black, and the paint had run and hardened into little stalactites along the bird's wings, making it look like a bat.

The gate opened by itself, and as she went through Fliss heard a voice that whispered, 'The Gate of Fate.' She was drawn along a short pathway and up some stone steps to the front door, which also opened by itself. 'The Keep of Sleep,' whispered the voice.

The door closed silently behind her. Moonlight shone coldly through a stained-glass panel into a gloomy hallway. At the far end were stairs that went up into blackness. She didn't want to climb that stairway but her feet drew her along the hallway and up.

She came to a landing with doors. The stairs took a turn and went on up. As Fliss climbed, it grew colder. There was another landing, more doors and another turn in the stairs. Upward to a third landing, then a fourth, and then there were no more stairs. She was at the top of the house. There were four doors, each with a number. 10. 11. 12. 13. As she read the numbers, door thirteen swung inward with a squeal. 'No!' she whispered, but it was no use. Her feet carried her over the threshold and the voice hissed, 'The Room of Doom.'

In the room was a table. On the table stood a long, pale box. Fliss thought she knew what it was. It filled her with horror, and she whimpered helplessly as her feet drew her towards it. When she was close she saw a shape in the box and there was a smell like damp earth. When she was very close the voice whispered, 'The Bed of Dread,' and then the shape sat up and reached out for her and she screamed. Her screams woke her and she lay damp and trembling in her bed.

Her mother came and switched on the light and looked down at her. 'What is it, Felicity? I thought I heard you scream.'

Fliss nodded. 'I had a dream, Mum. A nightmare.'

'Poor Fliss.' Her mother sat down on the bed and stroked her hair. 'It's all the excitement, I expect, thinking about going away tomorrow.' She smiled. 'Try to go back to sleep, dear. You've a long day ahead you.'

Fliss clutched her mother's arm. 'I don't want to go, Mum.'

'What?'

'I don't want to go. I want to drop out of the trip.'

'But why – not just because of a silly dream, surely?'

'Well, yes, I suppose so, Mum. It was about Whitby, I think. A house by the sea.'

'A house?'

'Yes.' She shivered, remembering. 'I was in this house and something horrible was after me. Can I drop out, Mum?'

Her mother sighed. 'I suppose you could, Felicity, if you're as upset as all that. I could ring Mrs Evans first thing, tell her not to expect you, but you might feel differently in the morning.' She smiled. 'Daylight makes us forget our dreams, or else they seem funny – even the scary ones. Let's decide in the morning, eh?'

Fliss smiled wanly 'OK.' She knew she wouldn't forget her dream, and that it would never seem funny. But it was all right. She was in control of her feet (she wiggled them under the covers to make sure), and they weren't going to take her anywhere she didn't want to go.

From *Room 13* by Robert Swindells

Examining the story

What happens?

Start by thinking about what actually happens in the extract.

- Fliss **dreams** about a strange house by the sea.
- Fliss **goes into** Room 13.
- Fliss **sees a strange box** with someone or something in it.
- Fliss **wakes up** from her nightmare.
- Her **mum comforts her**, but Fliss decides she doesn't want to go to Whitby.

Introduction: paragraph 1

Build up / development: paragraphs 2–7

Climax: paragraphs 8 and 9

Conclusion / resolution: paragraphs 10–13.

Structure of the story

Most stories follow a similar structure. The whole novel follows this structure, but the opening chapter on page 26 also follows the same structure, **as shown in the flow diagram on the left**.

However, the first chapter of the novel only provides a short-term resolution. There are many questions left unanswered, and this is what makes people want to read on.

Main character

Fliss is the main character in both the story and in this first chapter. We learn quite a lot about her and what to expect from her as the novel progresses:

- she has a vivid imagination
- she is frightened by the dream: *then the shape sat up and reached out for her and she screamed. Her screams woke her and she lay damp and trembling in her bed.*
- she doesn't want to go on the school trip
- she likes to be in control of what she is doing: *She was in control of her feet (she wiggled them under the covers to make sure), and they weren't going to take her anywhere she didn't want to go.*
- she is not easily convinced by her mum's explanation.

Setting

The setting for this chapter is mainly within Fliss's dream. It is set in an old house by the sea at night time. Fliss is convinced that her dream was about Whitby – this is important as it **gives us a clue** that the rest of the story will be set in Whitby. It also hints that the frightening setting of her dream will be revisited.

There are a number of elements that make the setting seem frightening:

- **circumstances**: it is dark and she is alone
- **descriptions**: a tall house *looming blackly*; *Moonlight shone coldly . . . into a gloomy hallway*; stairs that went up into *blackness*
- **choice of adjectives**: *dark, alone, afraid, black, gloomy.*

The adjectives help to create the frightening atmosphere / setting. They add detail, helping the reader to imagine what the house looked like.

What next?

Fliss tells her mum that she isn't going to Whitby with the rest of Year 7, but everything about the opening chapter suggests that she will go. Fliss is obviously the main character and her dream is given so much prominence in this chapter that it must be important to the rest of the story. We are kept guessing as to why her dream is so important and the only way to find out is to read the rest of the novel. This kind of **hook** is a good way to open a novel.

Word level

Adverbs: an adverb is a describing word. It describes how a verb is done. Many adverbs end in **-ly**. Often, an adverb can be formed by adding **-ly** to an adjective: black**ly**, cold**ly**, silent**ly**.

Progress Check

1 Which room does Fliss go into in her dream?
2 What is Fliss's full name?
3 What technique is used when the whispering voice speaks, *Bed of dread. . .* and so on?

1 Room 13   2 Felicity   3 Rhyme

2.5 Shakespeare

Themes

All of Shakespeare's plays explore particular ideas or issues that recur and develop as the play progresses. These ideas and issues are known as the **themes** of the play.

Shakespeare's plays cover the same themes as any modern piece of writing:

- love
- jealousy
- ambition
- family conflicts
- murder and intrigue
- revenge.

When you are studying a Shakespeare play, you should think about what the themes are and how they are revealed and developed.

Structure

Most plays follow a similar pattern of development, and Shakespeare's plays are no exception.

> Introduction to characters

↓

> Problems emerge and confusion occurs / themes are introduced

↓

> Chaos follows and themes are developed / we learn more about characters through their actions

↓

> Further development of themes

↓

> Climax of the play: **tragedy** – deaths occur; **comedy** – confusions are resolved and often marriages occur

↓

> Order is re-established

Understanding Shakespeare's language

Key Point	Hearing Shakespeare's language read aloud helps you to understand the meaning. Try to see a live performance or a film version of the play you are studying.

Rhyme and rhythm

There are different types of rhyme and rhythm in Shakespeare's plays.

- **Blank verse** – this is unrhymed lines of **iambic pentameter** (10 syllables alternately unstressed and stressed). Shakespeare wrote his plays in blank verse because it is versatile, it is not restricted by rhyme and it is the closest to the **natural rhythms of speech**. This makes it easy to create different moods, such as anger, love, and so on.
- **Iambic pentameter** – this term describes the number of **syllables** and **stresses** in a line, which is known as the **meter**. A **foot** is a pair of syllables. An iambic foot is an unstressed syllable followed by a stressed syllable. **There are five iambic feet in iambic pentameter**. Look at the example below, from Shakespeare's *Henry V* Act 1, scene 1, lines 67–69:

> **Canterbury:**
> It <u>must</u> / be <u>so</u>, / for <u>mir</u> / ac<u>les</u> / are <u>ceas'd</u>,
> And <u>there</u> / fore <u>we</u> / must <u>needs</u> / ad<u>mit</u> / the <u>means</u>,
> How <u>things</u> / are <u>per</u> / fec<u>ted</u>./

- **Rhyming couplets** – sometimes Shakespeare wrote in different styles for contrast. More **formal** and **traditional characters** making important speeches sometimes speak in rhyming couplets (the lines rhyme in pairs). Because of the constraint of finding rhymes, there is less movement and freedom in these speeches. This reflects the characters' formality. Look at the example below, from Shakespeare's *Romeo & Juliet* Act 1, scene 2, lines 24–25:

> **Capulet:** At my poor house look to behold this night
> Earth-treading stars that make dark heaven light:

Sometimes Shakespeare used a rhyming couplet to **round off** an important speech or scene. He also used rhyming couplets to **create** a particular kind of **atmosphere** or to present a character or event in a different way. The witches in *Macbeth* (Act 1, scene 1, lines 1–2) speak in rhyming couplets, and Shakespeare doesn't use iambic pentameter for their speeches.

> When shall we three meet again
> In thunder, lightning or in rain?

- **Prose** – the 'low characters', servants for example, speak in prose rather than verse. This reflects that they have less education and their subject matter is often low or coarse.

> **Trincolo:** I shall laugh myself to death at this puppy headed monster. A most scurvy monster: I could find in my heart to beat him –
>
> From Shakespeare's *The Tempest* Act 2, scene 2 lines 140–142

> **Porter:** Marry, sir, nose-painting, sleep, and urine.
>
> From Shakespeare's *Macbeth* Act 2, scene 3, line 27

Other characters sometimes speak in prose rather than verse. The important thing to remember is that Shakespeare always used blank verse, rhymed verse and prose for a particular reason.

How to read Shakespeare aloud

Key Point

If you are reading Shakespeare aloud, try to **read to the punctuation**. This will help with the sense of what you are reading.

Shakespeare's language is always much easier to understand when it is read well. Follow these tips.

- **Read to the punctuation** – if there is no punctuation at the end of a line then read straight through to the next line.
- **Don't rush** – speak clearly and think about what you are saying.
- **Words ending in 'd or -ed** – if a word is spelt 'd, e.g. **accus'd**, you pronounce it as we would say **accused**. However, if it is spelt **accused** in the text you pronounce the **-ed** as a separate syllable: **accuse-ed**.
- **Think about the tone of voice you should use.**
- **Think about what your character would do when saying the lines.**
- **Emphasise the words you think are most important** – the natural stresses of iambic pentameter should help you to do this.

Word level

Since Shakespeare's time there have been many changes to the English language, both in the way it is written and in the way it is spoken. The table on page 31 shows you the Shakespearian and modern English forms of some common words.

Thee.. thou.. who?	
Shakespeare	**Modern English**
art	are
hadst	had
hence	here
ill	bad
o'er	over
thee	you
thou	you used with someone very close to you or as an insult
you	you a more distant way of speaking to someone
thy	your
whence	where (from)
wither	where (to)
wouldst	would

Progress Check

1. Is the climax of a tragedy most likely to be a death or a marriage?
2. Does blank verse have 8, 10 or 12 syllables in each line?
3. The word *turn'd* should be pronounced with -ed as an extra syllable. TRUE or FALSE?

1 A death 2 10 3 False

Shakespeare's language – *Macbeth*

Key Point

Soliloquy – a character is alone on stage and speaks his or her thoughts aloud. Playwrights use this device to give the audience important information about the character and their motives that other characters in the play are unaware of.

AF5 AF6 AF7
You should be able to analyse the language, form and dramatic impact of scenes and plays by published dramatists / playwrights.

The story so far: the witches have predicted that Macbeth will be King; he and his wife have planned to murder King Duncan. In the following soliloquy, Macbeth is having second thoughts.

> He's here in **double trust**;
> First as I am **his kinsman** and his **subject**,
> Strong both against the deed; then as **his host**,
> Who should against his murderer shut the door,   15
> Not bear the knife myself. Besides this Duncan
> Hath borne his faculties so **meek**, hath been
> So **clear** in his great office, that his virtues
> Will plead like angels, **trumpet-tongued** against

> The **deep damnation** of his **taking-off** 20
> And pity, like a **naked newborn babe**
> striding the blast, or heaven's cherubin horsed
> Upon the sightless couriers of the air,
> Shall blow **the horrid deed** in every eye,
> That tears shall drown the wind. I have no spur 25
> To prick the sides of my intent, but only
> **Vaulting ambition which o'erleaps itself**
> **and falls on th'other –**
>
> *Macbeth* Act 1, scene 7, lines 12–28

Lines 12–16

- The phrase *double trust* emphasises that Macbeth would be breaking Duncan's trust twice. He sets out the reasons logically:
  1a he is his *kinsman* (relative)
  1b he is a trusted *subject*
  2 Duncan is a guest in Macbeth's house, so he should protect him, not plan to kill him.
- Macbeth presents himself with a **well-reasoned argument** against the murder plan.

Lines 16–18

- These lines are more **emotive**. Macbeth reminds himself of all Duncan's qualities. Words like *meek* and *clear* are used to show that Duncan is virtuous and without sin.

Line 20

- **Duncan's goodness** is **contrasted** with the *deep damnation* of the act of murder. This is a direct comparison of the spiritual state of the two men, Duncan and Macbeth, his killer. Macbeth realises that he would be damned for eternity for such a sinful act.

Lines 21–25

- He uses images of innocence and purity – the **newborn baby** and the **cherubin** (the highest order of angels) – as the messengers of Duncan's death. He imagines that the winds will be drowned with tears. This emphasises the scale of public mourning for the death of such a king.

Lines 25–28

- In comparison with all the reasons not to kill Duncan, Macbeth's only reason to carry out the murder is his ambition. He **compares** his ambition to a horse that tries to jump too high and falls on the other side of the fence. Macbeth thinks that if he gives in to ambition, he will fail in the end.
- Alliteration is used for emphasis in this speech: *trumpet-tongued*, *deep damnation*, *naked newborn babe*.

AF5

Euphemism – a mild or inoffensive way of expressing something unpleasant, frightening or offensive.

In this speech Macbeth lists all the reasons why he shouldn't murder Duncan. Throughout the soliloquy he uses **euphemisms** for the murder, e.g. *bear the knife*, *his taking-off*, *horrid deed*. This shows that Macbeth is reluctant to think about the brutality of the act of murder. He is trying to avoid the reality of the situation and cannot face up to the evil nature of the plan that he and his wife have made.

Shakespeare's language – *Romeo and Juliet*

Key Point	Oxymoron – two terms used together that directly contradict each other.

This is an extract from *Romeo and Juliet* (Act 1 sc. i ll.178–85). Romeo is in love with a woman from a family that his family hate. When he arrives on the scene, he finds that the families have been fighting again.

> O me! – What fray was here?
> Yet tell me not, for I have heard it all.
> Here's much to do with hate, but more with love:– 180
> Why then, O brawling love! O loving hate!
> anything, of nothing first created!
> heavy lightness! serious vanity!
> Misshapen chaos of well-seeming forms!
> Feather of lead, bright smoke, cold fire, sick health! 185

Lines 178–9

- Romeo is surprised by the violent scene he sees. He asks for an explanation but then realises that it is the same conflict that always happens. We can tell he is unhappy and that he doesn't like the fighting.

Line 180

- He mentions love and hate in the same line, this shows he is confused because he loves a woman he should hate.

Line 181

- The reversal of brawling love and loving hate, emphasises his confusion.

Lines 183–5

- The list of oxymorons again emphasise his confusion and conflicting feelings; he is unhappy when he should be happy (in love) and in love where he should hate. All of the contradictions are negative, which shows that he is depressed and unhappy. This is because Rosaline, the woman he loves, will not return his love.

The fact that Romeo talks only about his feelings and lists the oxymorons in such a dramatic way shows that he is caught up in his own feelings. You might even think that he is almost enjoying torturing himself and wallowing in his misery.

This extract from later on in the play (Act 3 sc.i ll.126–33) shows Romeo furious and ready to fight. He has married Juliet secretly. Her cousin, Tybalt, wants to fight him but he refuses, saying he loves Tybalt. When Tybalt kills Romeo's best friend, his mood changes.

> Alive! in triumph! and Mercutio slain!
> Away to heaven respective lenity,
> And fire-ey'd fury be my conduct now! -
> Now, Tybalt, take the villain back again,
> That late thou gav'st me; for Mercutio's soul   130
> Is but a little way above our heads,
> Staying for thine to keep him company:
> Either thou or I, or both, must go with him.

Line 126

- The exclamation marks show that Romeo is angry. They also mark the three circumstances that fuel his anger. If Mercutio is dead then Tybalt shouldn't be alive or triumphant.

Line 127

- As he is now related to Tybalt, it is **proper** that he should **forgive** him anything – this is the meaning of **respective lenity**. He shouts for these proper feelings to go away. He wants to be angry and out of control.

Line 128

- **Fire ey'd fury** is like the modern day expression "seeing red". Romeo wants to be ruled by his anger and blinded by rage, he does not want to see the consequences of his actions. If he thought about it, he wouldn't be able to continue – he is about to kill his wife's cousin.

Lines 130–2

- When he says that Mercutio is waiting (staying) for Tybalt to keep him company, he is reminding himself of why he has to act.

Line 133

He says that either Tybalt or himself or both of them will have to die. This shows that he is prepared to fight to the death for his friend's memory.

The whole tone of this speech is angry. The language used shows Romeo trying to make himself more and more angry so he can put the consequences out of his mind.

He mentions heaven but he sends his "proper feelings" there. **Fire ey'd fury** is more appropriate to hell; perhaps he feels his behaviour will condemn him to hell if he does kill Tybalt. **Remember** that religion and the consequences of sin were very important in Shakespeare's time.

Shakespeare's language – *The Tempest*

Caliban curses Prospero and says that the spirits under Prospero's control torment him for every little thing he does wrong.

> CALIBAN   All the **infections** that the sun sucks up
> From **bogs**, **fens**, **flats**, on Prosper fall, **and make him**
> **By inch-meal a disease**. His spirits hear me,
> And yet I needs must curse. But they'll nor **pinch**,
> **Fright me** with urchin-shows, **pitch me i'th'mire**,
> Nor **lead me like a firebrand in the dark**
> **Out of my way**, unless he bid 'em; but
> For every **trifle** are they set upon me,
> Sometime like apes, that mow and chatter at me
> And after **bite me**; then like hedgehogs, which
> Lie tumbling in my barefoot way and **mount**
> **Their pricks at my footfall**; sometime am I
> **All wound with adders**, who with cloven tongues
> **Do hiss me into madness**.
>
> *The Tempest* Act 2, scene 2, lines 1–14

Lines 1–3

- Caliban's hatred is emphasised by the **listing device** used in line two; he wants to draw up 'infections' from as many places as he can – *bogs*, *fens*, *flats*. Rather than wishing Prospero to suffer from a disease, he wants to *make him ... a disease*. This together with the idea of him being consumed by it inch by inch *by inch-meal*, suggests that Caliban enjoys the idea of Prospero being made to suffer as much as possible.

Lines 4–7

- Caliban begins to list all the terrible things that Prospero tells his spirit to do to him. At first the emphasis is on mental rather than physical cruelty. They confuse him, frighten him and lead him astray.

Line 8

- The word *trifle* is used to emphasise the fact that he feels he is punished for very minor offences.

Lines 9–14

- The **effect** of these lines is to **build up** the range of tortures used and **reflect** the fact that Caliban's rage and fear are **building up** under this relentless torment. This list of torments focuses more on the physical dangers he faces – being bitten by apes, pricked by hedgehogs and crushed by adders. The overall effect is revisited in the final line of this section when Caliban claims to be *hiss[ed] into madness*.

Progress Check

1. A character delivers a soliloquy when there are no other characters on stage. TRUE / FALSE
2. An oxymoron is a contradiction. TRUE / FALSE
3. Religion wasn't very important in Shakespeare's time. TRUE / FALSE

1 True 2 True 3 False

Assessment questions

The following questions will help you to prepare for the **Optional Tests** or **APP Tasks**.

Read the extract below and answer the questions that follow.

We had no torch. The light that came through the chinks in the boards was pale and weak. We blundered through the dark.

We held hands and stretched our free hands out in front us. We walked into the wall. We caught our toes on loose floorboards. We stumbled as we climbed the stairs. We shuffled across the first landing. We felt for the handle of the door to the room where we thought we'd left Skellig. We inched the door open. We whispered, 'Skellig! Skellig!' No answer. We moved forward carefully, arms outstretched, feeling forward with our feet before we took each step. Our breath was fast, shallow, trembly. My heart was thundering. I opened my eyes wide, glared into the dark, seeking the shape of his body on the floor. Nothing there, just the blankets, the pillow, the plastic dish, the beer bottle rolling away from my stumbling feet.

'Where is he?' whispered Mina.

'Skellig,' we whispered. 'Skellig! Skellig!'

We turned back to the landing again, we stumbled up the next flight of stairs, we opened many doors, we stared past them into pitch black rooms, we whispered his name, we heard nothing but our own breath, our own uncertain feet, his name echoing back to us from bare floorboards and bare walls, we turned back to the landing again, we stumbled up the next flight of stairs.

From *Skellig* by David Almond

1. Find **three** examples of **verbs** used to describe the characters' movement. What effect do these words have? **(AF5)**
2. Describe the structure of the final sentence. Why is this effective? **(AF5)**
3. What techniques are used to create a feeling of fear and tension in this extract? **(AF5)**

Re-read the extract on pages 22–23 from *A Kestrel for a Knave* and then answer the question below.
1. How does the author create a feeling of sympathy for Billy Casper? **(AF6)**

The following questions test your understanding of a Shakespeare play you have studied. Some questions relate to specific plays whilst others are general and can be applied to any Shakespeare play. The extracts are not provided so you will need your own copy of the play you have studied. These questions target AFs 5–7.

Romeo and Juliet: Act 1 scene 1 lines 98–end, and Act 2 scene 2 lines 1–157
1. How does Shakespeare show the difference between Romeo's love for Rosaline and his love for Juliet in these scenes?
    You should write about:
    - The language Romeo uses in the two scenes.
    - The way love makes him feel in the two scenes.
    - How he responds to what Juliet says.

The Tempest: Act 1 scene 2 lines 376–end, and Act 3 scene 1
2. How does Shakespeare use the character of Prospero to show the sincerity of Ferdinand and Miranda's love?
    You should write about:
    - How Ferdinand and Miranda behave and what they say when they first see each other.
    - What Prospero does to test their love.
    - How they respond to Prospero's behaviour.
    - The way the characters have changed between the two scenes.

Assessment questions

Macbeth: Act 1 scene 7, and Act 4 scene 1 lines 47–104

3. How much influence do the female characters in these scenes have over Macbeth's thoughts and actions?

   You should write about:

   - What Macbeth says when he is alone.
   - How Lady Macbeth persuades Macbeth to go ahead with the murder.
   - The way Macbeth interprets the apparitions.
   - Who you feel is most responsible for Macbeth's actions.

Twelfth Night: Act 1 scene 1, and Act 3 scene 1 lines 78–end

4. How does Shakespeare use Orsino and Olivia to explore the idea of unrequited love?

   You should write about:

   - The language they use to describe their feelings.
   - The way their feelings make them behave.
   - How the audience might respond to these characters.
   - Whether you think they are really in love.

Henry V: Act 2 scene 2 line 76–end, and Act 3 scene 1 and scene 2 lines 1–27

5. How does Shakespeare reveal the depth of Henry V's character in these scenes?

   You should write about:

   - The way he deals with the traitors.
   - What he says to Scroop.
   - The way he *rallies* his troops.
   - What the behaviour of other characters reveals about the King.

General

6. Comment on the behaviour of the main character(s) in two key scenes from the Shakespeare play you have studied.

   You should write about:

   - The language they use.
   - The way they behave towards other characters.
   - How their character(s) change or develop between the two scenes.

7. How are relationships developed in two key scenes from the Shakespeare play you have studied?

   You should write about:

   - The language the characters use.
   - The way characters behave towards each other.
   - The way events in the play have affected their relationship.

8. How would you direct two key scenes from the Shakespeare play you have studied to create an appropriate atmosphere?

   You should:

   - Give direction about how characters should behave.
   - Give direction about how lines should be spoken.
   - Give explanation about why a particular atmosphere is required.

3 Reading poetry

After studying this section you should be able to:

- understand poetry that tells a story
- comment on the use of imagery in poetry
- comment on the structure of a poem
- comment on and understand pre-1914 poetry
- compare poems on the same theme

To achieve the following National Curriculum levels you need to do the following for each level.

Level 4
- Understand what the poem is about.
- Understand the **ideas and feelings** in the poem.

Level 5
- Begin to look for layers of **meaning** beneath the surface of the text.
- Notice the effects of **particular words and phrases**.

Level 6
- Comment on the effective use of words and phrases and particular **devices of language**.
- Locate and comment on the **use of imagery**.

Level 7
- Comment on the **structure of the poem**.
- Trace development within a poem.
- Give a **personal response** to the poem and what you think the poet has achieved.

3.1 Poetry that tells a story

Understanding poetry

You shouldn't expect to understand everything about a poem after a first reading; it will be packed full of emotions, ideas and images. Reading a poem involves detective work – you have to look closely under the surface for clues.

Try reading a poem through **three times**, each time looking for a different set of clues:

- **First reading** – the general meaning and story line of the poem (if it has one).
- **Second reading** – feelings and emotions contained in the poem.
- **Third reading** – interesting images contained in the poem.

Ballads

A **ballad** is a poem that **tells a story**. It is a **traditional** kind of poetry that began as an oral storytelling form. The stories were told in **rhyme** so that they were easier to remember without being written down. Ballads still follow a lot of the same conventions now:

- tell a story
- strong, regular rhythm and rhyme
- repeated lines or refrains (**chorus**)
- often have a moral.

'**What Has Happened to Lulu?**' *by Charles Causley*

What has happened to Lulu, mother?
    What has happened to Lu?
There's **nothing in her bed** but an old rag doll
And by its side a shoe.

Why is her **window wide**, mother,
    The curtain flapping free,
And only a circle on the dusty shelf
    Where her **money-box** used to be?

Why do you turn your head, mother,
    And why do the tear-drops fall?
And why do you crumple that **note** on the fire
    And say it is nothing at all?

I woke to hear voices late last night,
    I heard **an engine roar**,
Why do you tell me the things I heard
    Were a dream and nothing more?

I heard somebody **cry**, mother,
    In anger or in pain,
But now I ask you why, mother,
    You say it was a gust of rain.

Why do you **wander about** as though
    You don't know what to do?
What has happened to Lulu, mother?
    What has happened to Lu?

Key Point

When you study a new poem you should read it three times. Look for:
- the **general meaning**
- **feelings** and **emotions**
- **interesting images**.

The story

The way the poem 'What has happened to Lulu?' is written allows the reader to piece the story together stanza by stanza. There is a **clue** in each one:

1. empty bed
2. open window and missing money-box
3. note
4. engine roar late at night
5. crying
6. mum distracted.

The child's sister has run away. Mother doesn't want to talk about it and the child is trying to find out what happened.

Solving a mystery

The next poem only tells part of a story, it **reveals a mystery**. The poem raises as many questions as it answers. As you read the poem, think about the **questions** that it raises and the information that isn't supplied.

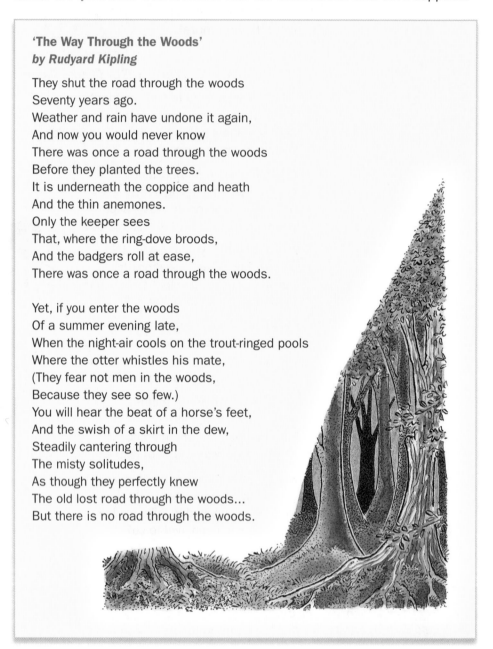

'**The Way Through the Woods**'
by Rudyard Kipling

They shut the road through the woods
Seventy years ago.
Weather and rain have undone it again,
And now you would never know
There was once a road through the woods
Before they planted the trees.
It is underneath the coppice and heath
And the thin anemones.
Only the keeper sees
That, where the ring-dove broods,
And the badgers roll at ease,
There was once a road through the woods.

Yet, if you enter the woods
Of a summer evening late,
When the night-air cools on the trout-ringed pools
Where the otter whistles his mate,
(They fear not men in the woods,
Because they see so few.)
You will hear the beat of a horse's feet,
And the swish of a skirt in the dew,
Steadily cantering through
The misty solitudes,
As though they perfectly knew
The old lost road through the woods...
But there is no road through the woods.

The following questions are raised in the poem.

- **Why** did 'they' shut the road?
- **Who** are 'they'?
- **Why** do so few men go into the woods?
- **Who** does the skirt that swishes belong to?

Progress Check

1. Which lines of the first poem are repeated?
2. Is the rhyme scheme of the second poem **regular** or **irregular**?
3. Which ballad feature does the second poem have?

1 Lines 1 and 2   2 Regular   3 Repeated lines

3.2 Imagery

Read the poem printed below. It makes use of one particular kind of imagery. Can you work out what it is? You could use the **glossary** on pages 153–156 to help you.

'**City Jungle**' *by Pie Corbett*

Rain splinters town.

Lizard cars cruise by;
their radiators grin.

Thin headlights stare –
shop doorways keep
their mouths shut.

At the roadside
hunched houses cough.
Newspapers shuffle by,
hands in their pockets.
The gutter gargles.

A motorbike snarls;
dustbins flinch.

Streetlights bare
their yellow teeth.
The motorway's cat-black tongue
lashes across
the glistening back
of the tarmac night.

Personification

Throughout this poem, the poet uses **personification** to bring the city he describes to life.

Most of the personification is created through the poet's choice of **verbs** – *grin*, *stare*, *flinch*, *cough*. The objects described perform human or animal actions and this makes them appear to be living creatures.

The poet also uses some carefully chosen **nouns** to add to the effect of personification. The shop doorways become *mouths* in shop front faces and the newspapers put their *hands* in their *pockets*.

Key Point

Personification is an image that brings an inanimate object to life by giving it human qualities.
Alliteration is the term for a group of words that all begin with the same letter.

Painting pictures with words

The poet uses personification to create a **threatening atmosphere**. The city is described at night when, in the darkness, inanimate objects come to life and rule the city.

The cars and motorbikes are presented as arrogant and aggressive, like bullies. The dustbins, which rattle because of the vibrations made by the motorbike's engine, become the innocent victims of the bullies.

A motorbike snarls;
Dustbins flinch.

The phrase *hunched houses* makes you think of terraced houses very close together. The fact that they are *coughing* suggests that they are damp and cold; their chimneys could be smoking.

The description of the newspapers is very effective. These newspapers have been read and thrown away and are blowing around in the wind. The way the poet describes them makes them sound like people keeping their heads down, trying to get home and ignoring the bullies.

Newspapers shuffle by,
Hands in their pockets.

Progress Check

1 What technique is used in the lines *hunched houses cough* and *The gutter gargles*?
2 How would you describe the structure of the poem? a) It has a regular rhythm and rhyme scheme. b) It is written in free verse (no regular rhythm or rhyme scheme).
3 Why is the title of the poem effective?

1 Alliteration   2 b) Free verse   3 It makes the city sound alive, dangerous and unfamiliar.

Simile and metaphor

Read the two poems that follow. Can you identify the **simile** and the **metaphor**?

> **From 'The Farmer's Bride'** *by Charlotte Mew*
>
> She does the work about the house
> As well as most, but **like a mouse**:
>   Happy enough to chat and play
>   With birds and rabbits and such as they,
> So long as men-folk stay away.
> "Not near, not near!" her eyes beseech
> When one of us comes within reach.

> **From 'Valentine'** *by Carol Ann Duffy*
>
> Not a red rose or a satin heart.
>
> I give you an onion.
> **It is a moon wrapped in brown paper.**

Key Point

Don't confuse similes and metaphors. A **simile** is a comparison of two objects using the words **like** or **as**. A **metaphor** states that one object **is** another object, **without** making a **comparison**.

Similes

The highlighted section of 'The Farmer's Bride' is a **simile**. The poet describes the farmer's wife as being *like a mouse* because she gets on with the housework very quietly. But the poem suggests that she is only quiet and timid with *men-folk*; she is happy to *chat and play* with animals. The comparison of her to an animal highlights the fact that she is more comfortable with *birds and rabbits and such as they* than she is with *men-folk*, like her husband.

Metaphors

The highlighted section of 'Valentine' is a **metaphor**. This is effective because it's an unusual way to describe an onion, but when you think carefully about the physical qualities of an onion it makes perfect sense. Think about the colour and texture of an onion skin – it is just like brown paper. The onion itself is round, it reflects light and it is the same colour as the moon.

Making an unusual connection between the moon and an onion is also effective because the poem is about an unusual gift. It is about giving an onion as a valentine gift instead of a traditional card or roses.

Traditionally, the moon and moonlight are connected to romance and love – describing the onion in this way connects it to the subject of the poem.

Progress Check

1. Is a comparison of two different objects or ideas using the words *like* or *as* a **simile** or a **metaphor**?
2. **Personification** is a type of metaphor. TRUE or FALSE?

1 Simile   2 True

3.3 Structure

AF7
You should be able to explore how **form contributes to meaning** in poems from different times and cultures.

The structure of a poem is very important. A writer can create many different effects with rhyme, rhythm, shape, line length and stanza form. In the Japanese poetry form, **haiku**, structure is the most important feature.

The structure of a haiku poem is always the same:
- **three lines**
- **first line five syllables**
- **second line seven syllables**
- **final line five syllables**.

This kind of structure doesn't allow for expansive imagery; instead, a brief, striking impression of nature is created.

> A dark storm rages
> Low over the wintry moors
> And strikes the bare earth.

Studying the structure of a poem

The next poem is about a memory the poet has of when she was a young girl. A little girl nearly drowned in the lake and the poet's mother resuscitated her. But in the fourth verse, the poet wonders if it was a real event or if she was simply remembering a picture she had once seen of a drowning girl.

When you read this poem, you should pay particular attention to the **structure**. Some of the important features have been highlighted for you.

'Cold Knap Lake'
by Gillian Clarke

Time

We **once** watched a crowd
pull a drowned child from the lake.
Blue-lipped and dressed in water's long green silk
she lay for dead.

Then kneeling on the earth,
a heroine, her red head bowed,
her wartime cotton frock soaked,
my mother gave a stranger's child her breath.
The crowd stood silent,
drawn by the dread of it.

The child breathed, bleating
and rosy in my mother's hands.
My father took her home to a poor house
and watched her thrashed for almost drowning.

Short sentence

Long sentence

Was I there?
Or is that troubled surface something else
shadowy under the dipped fingers of willows
where satiny mud blooms in cloudiness
after the treading, heavy webs of swans
as their wings beat and whistle on the air?

All lost things lie under closing water
in that lake with the poor man's daughter.

Rhyme, rhythm and stanza length

The poem has a regular pattern for the most part. It consists of five stanzas. The first four stanzas follow a regular pattern of four lines then six lines, then four lines then six lines. However, the final stanza breaks the pattern as it consists of only two lines.

The lines vary in length throughout the poem, with the final two-line stanza forming a rhyming couplet. This rhyming couplet is the only rhyme in the whole poem and it helps to emphasise the point made in the final lines. The stanzas include half rhyme, for example, *earth* and *breath*, but there is no full rhyme in the poem until the final stanza.

When read aloud, the poem has an irregular rhythm. The lines in each stanza tend to run on, building up to the main focus of the stanza.

Time

The poem tells a story and is related in a very factual way. In the first stanza, the poet sets the scene, but simply uses the word *once* to describe when the incident took place. In the second stanza, the poet moves the story along using the word *then*, and describing how her mother, the *heroine*, brought the little girl back to life. The third stanza goes on to describe what happened after the little girl had been resuscitated.

In the fourth stanza, the poet brings time back to the present, as she wonders whether the incident actually took place at all or whether it was just in her imagination.

The final two-line stanza could be interpreted in a number of ways: memories can easily be lost and altered with time; we see things through our own perspective as time passes – our memories are not always reliable.

Sentence structure

The first stanza consists of two straightforward sentences over four lines. These sentences are not particularly short or long, but they set the story clearly and simply.

In the second stanza, the first four lines make up one long sentence, which builds up the tension and the urgency of the scene as the poet's mother attempts to resuscitate the girl. The structure of this sentence also allows the poet to withhold, until the end of the sentence, the fact that the heroine is her own mother. This also creates more drama.

The third stanza, in a similar pattern to the first, contains two sentences over four lines.

The fourth stanza begins with an abrupt question: *Was I there?*, which contrasts sharply to the following 36-word sentence, as the poet tries to answer her own question. This answer is given as one very long sentence over five lines, which highlights her confusion. This is also contrasted with the shorter final sentence in the fifth stanza.

The technique of **enjambment** within the stanzas keeps each stage of the story moving forward, without breaking up the action with unnecessary full stops. Where full stops are used, they prove to be very effective in providing a close to that part of the story, for example, at the end of the first stanza.

Progress Check

1 How many syllables are there in the first line of the fourth stanza?
2 How does the rest of the fourth stanza compensate for this?
3 What effect does the first line of the fourth stanza have on the rhythm of the stanza?

1 3 2 The rest of the stanza consists of one very long sentence, containing many more syllables. This balances out the three-syllable line, which stands out in the poem as being very short. 3 It breaks up the flow of the stanza because it is so abrupt. It contrasts with the rest of the stanza and means the rhythm has to build up again throughout the rest of the stanza.

3.4 Pre-1914 poetry – William Blake

AF7
You should be able to identify links between literary heritage texts and their times.

William Blake wrote two books of poetry between 1785 and 1795 called *Songs of Innocence* and *Songs of Experience*. He was very concerned about social issues of the time, such as chimney sweep boys, the poor and the power of the church. He used his poetry to express his concerns to the public. The *Songs of Innocence* show the world how it could or should be, and the *Songs of Experience* show what Blake thought the world was really like.

Language differences

You may find that writing from another historical period is difficult to understand at first. **Sentence structure and word order** may be more complicated and some words may seem unfamiliar. However, with concentration and perseverance you should be able to overcome these difficulties.

Key Point

Here are some tips for overcoming differences in language.
- Use a dictionary.
- Check for apostrophes: *'twas* = it was, *where-e're* = where ever.
- Read the difficult lines out loud.
- Try changing the word order.

Reading the poems

Key Point

Remember to read the poems **three** times, looking for different clues each time.

The two poems called '**Holy Thursday**' were a complaint about the way orphan children were treated. As you read the poems, look for the differences in the way the people in the poems are presented.

Repetition of important words

> **'Holy Thursday' from *Songs of Innocence* by William Blake**
>
> 'Twas on a Holy Thursday, their **innocent** faces clean,
> The children walking two & two, in red & blue & green,
> Grey headed beadles walk'd before with wands as white as snow,
> Till into the high dome of Paul's they **like Thames' waters flow**.
>
> O what a multitude they seem'd, these **flowers of London town!**
> Seated in companies they sit with radiance all their own.
> The hum of multitudes was there, but multitudes of lambs,
> Thousands of little boys & girls raising their **innocent** hands.
>
> **Now like a mighty wind they raise to heaven the voice of song,**
> **Or like harmonious thunderings** the seats of heaven among.
> Beneath them sit the aged men, wise guardians of the poor;
> Then cherish pity, lest you drive an angel from your door.

Simile

Metaphor

'Holy Thursday' from *Songs of Experience* by William Blake

Is this a holy thing to see,
In a rich and fruitful land,
Babes reduc'd to misery,
Fed with cold and usurous hand?

Is that trembling cry a song?
Can it be a song of joy?
And so many children poor?
It is a land of poverty!

And their sun does never shine,
And their fields are bleak & bare,
And their ways are fill'd with thorns;
It is eternal winter there.

For where-e'er the sun does shine,
And where-e'er the rain does fall,
Babe can never hunger there,
Nor poverty the mind appall.

Comparing the poems

AF6
You should be able to trace the development of themes, ideas and values in texts.

The **first poem** is about the charity school children singing in St Paul's cathedral and giving thanks for the way they are looked after by the church elders. In this poem, the children are described in a positive way.

In the **second poem**, all the images and ideas are negative. Blake suggests that the first poem isn't really a true picture of the way the children are treated.

Vocabulary

- **Innocence** – in the first poem, the word *innocent* is used twice. This suggests that the children are harmless, that they need to be looked after and that anybody would be happy to take care of them.
- **Lambs** – in the first poem, the children are described as *lambs*, which links to the idea of innocence. The children are harmless and defenceless and the *wise guardians of the poor* look after them.
- *Poverty* – in the second poem, the word *poverty* is repeated. This suggests that the children have to go without comforts.
- *Bleak and bare* – in the second poem Blake creates the impression that everything is empty, cold and depressing. This contrasts with the bright colours of the first poem.

Imagery

Blake uses a range of images in the **first poem**:

- *The flowers of London town*

This **metaphor** is effective because it makes the children seem bright, cheerful and beautiful. People like to see flowers brightening up a town or city, and this image suggests that people like to see the children walking through the streets.

- *Like Thames' waters flow*

This **simile** is effective for many reasons:

  - the Thames is important to the life of the city and this makes the children seem important to the city
  - if you looked at the children from above, they might look like a river moving smoothly through the streets
  - this image gives you a good idea of how many children there are.

- Their songs are described as *like a mighty wind* and *harmonious thunderings*.

  - Using **similes** connected to the weather links the children to the innocence of nature.
  - Thunder and wind are both powerful forces, and using these images gives the impression that the children's singing is also very powerful.

Use of imagery is limited in the **second poem** because Blake wants to be more direct and straightforward in his comments about the situation the charity school children are in. Their songs are now described as a *trembling cry*.

In the third stanza Blake creates the image of their lives lived out in the *eternal winter*. The sun never shines, the trees and fields are bare. Their journey through life is made difficult by thorny obstacles.

The adults in the poems

The way the children are presented is linked to the way Blake sees the people who are supposed to look after the children. In the **first poem** the descriptions are positive:

- *Grey-headed beadles walk'd before with wands as white as snow*.

  - They are presented as the leaders, making sure the children go the right way.
  - The description is quite neutral, so they seem harmless themselves.
  - The simile *wands as white as snow* makes the reader think of innocence and purity.

- *Wise guardians of the poor*

  - In this description, the word *wise* suggests that they will always do the right thing.
  - A *guardian* looks after and protects somebody or something.

In the **second poem** the description of the men who 'look after' the children is negative:

- *Fed by cold usurous hand*. This description is effective for a number of reasons:

  - there isn't an actual person mentioned in this poem, which suggests that the children are the responsibility of a faceless organisation

- the word *cold* suggests a lack of care or concern
- **usury** is the practice of lending money at unfairly high interest rates. In this poem the use of the word *usurous* suggests meanness and greed. It also hints that money that should be used to help the children is being spent elsewhere.

Structure

Pre-1914 poetry tends to have **more formal structure** than later poetry.
- The **first poem** has three four-line stanzas. It is written in **rhyming couplets** and this makes the poem seem quite light-hearted and complete.
- The **second poem** is also written in four-line stanzas. However, the rhyme scheme is different. Although some of the lines rhyme and there is some patterning, **the rhyme is inconsistent** – this suits the tone of the poem.

Progress Check

1. There are lots of questions in the second poem. Why do you think this is?
2. How would we express *the seats of heaven among*?
3. What does *lest* mean?

1 It shows that he questions what happens to the children. 2 Amongst the seats of heaven. 3 In order not to.

3.5 Comparing poems on a theme or subject

War poetry

AF6
You should be able to compare the themes and style of at least two poets.

During the First World War, lots of soldiers wrote poetry in the trenches to record their feelings and fears. Much of this poetry is now recognised as some of the most powerful writing of the twentieth century.

Realism or patriotism?

Not all of the poets writing at this time had the same feelings about the war. The poetry written at this time falls into two broad categories:
- **realist** – the poets who wanted to represent the horror and grim reality of war
- **patriotic** – the poets who saw the war as a 'necessary evil' and who felt it was honourable and noble to be involved, and to die for your country if necessary.

Each of the following poems (on pages 50 and 51) represents one of these categories. As you read them, think about the **message** that each poet wants to deliver and how he tries to do this.

Key Point

Remember to read the poems **three** times, looking for different clues each time.

‘Dulce Et Decorum Est’
by Wilfred Owen

Bent double, like old beggars under sacks,
Knock-kneed, coughing like hags, we cursed through sludge,
Till on the haunting flares we turned our backs
And towards our distant rest began to trudge.
Men marched asleep. Many had lost their boots
But limped on, blood-shod. All went lame; all blind;

Drunk with fatigue; deaf even to the hoots
Of gas shells dropping softly behind.
GAS! GAS! quick, boys! – An ecstasy of fumbling,
Fitting the clumsy helmets just in time;
But someone still was yelling out and stumbling,
And flound'ring like a man in fire or lime. . .
Dim, through the misty panes and thick green light,
As under a green sea, I saw him drowning.

In all my dreams, before my helpless sight,
He plunges at me, guttering, choking, drowning.

If in some smothering dreams you too could pace
Behind the wagon that we flung him in,
And watch the white eyes writhing in his face,
His hanging face, like a devil's sick of sin;
If you could hear, at every jolt, the blood
Come gargling from the froth-corrupted lungs,
Obscene as cancer, bitter as the cud
Of vile, incurable sores on innocent tongues, –
My friend, you would not tell with such high zest
To children ardent for some desperate glory,
The old Lie: *Dulce et decorum est*
Pro patria mori.

Key Point

Dulce et decorum est pro patria mori is Latin, meaning ‘it is a sweet and honourable thing to die for your country’.

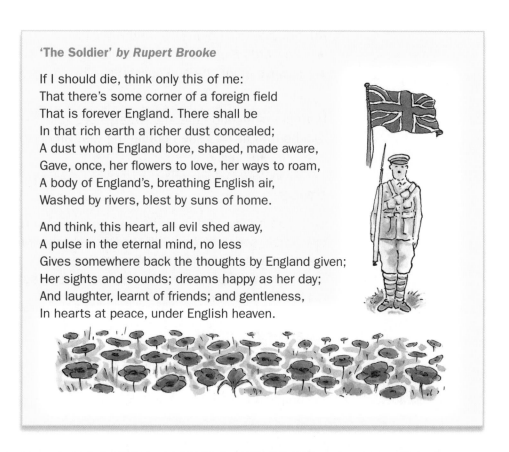

'The Soldier' *by Rupert Brooke*

If I should die, think only this of me:
That there's some corner of a foreign field
That is forever England. There shall be
In that rich earth a richer dust concealed;
A dust whom England bore, shaped, made aware,
Gave, once, her flowers to love, her ways to roam,
A body of England's, breathing English air,
Washed by rivers, blest by suns of home.

And think, this heart, all evil shed away,
A pulse in the eternal mind, no less
Gives somewhere back the thoughts by England given;
Her sights and sounds; dreams happy as her day;
And laughter, learnt of friends; and gentleness,
In hearts at peace, under English heaven.

Comparing the poems

Title

The title of the **first poem** is not immediately easy to understand. It links to the final lines of the poem, which declare that the sentiment expressed in this Latin phrase is a lie. The title is **ironic** because the whole poem sets out to prove that it isn't sweet and honourable to die for your country in this way.

The title of the **second poem**, 'The Soldier', is far more **straightforward**. In the poem this soldier expresses his thoughts about dying for his country.

Tone / attitude

Wilfred Owen was a **realist**. He clearly describes the **horror** of war in his poem and doesn't shy away from the terrible things that he has seen. He is keen that people at home should know exactly how terrible and frightening it is to be involved in the fighting.

Rupert Brooke was far more **patriotic** and more likely to agree with the Latin phrase in Owen's poem. Although the soldier doesn't claim to enjoy the war, he does seem proud to fight for his country. His message is that dying for England is a worthwhile reason for dying. He makes the idea of death seem quite **romantic and painless**.

Vocabulary

Wilfred Owen's poem contains lots of negative vocabulary:
- illness / disease – *coughing, vile sores, cancer, lame, blind*
- tiredness – *distant rest, fatigue, asleep*
- inability to breathe – *drowning, choking, guttering, smothering*.

Rupert Brooke's poem is far more positive:

● the words *England* or *English* are repeated six times
● positive emotions and concepts – **love, laughter, friendship, gentleness, peace, happiness**.

Both poets mention dreams. Owen's are *smothering dreams*, full of the real horrors he has seen during the war. Brooke's soldier refers to *dreams happy as her day*.

Voice

Both poems are written in the **first person**. Owen's poem is written in his own voice, speaking from bitter personal experience. This makes the terrible events he writes about seem very direct and real. Brooke's poem is written in the persona of a brave and proud soldier who feels he owes his life to his country.

Imagery

There are many **effective images** in **Wilfred Owen's** poem, which have been highlighted in the text. Read the poem again and try to explain why each image is effective. The first one has been done for you.

Owen uses two similes to show how tired and ill the soldiers are:

> **Bent double, like old beggars under sacks,**
> **Knock-kneed, coughing like hags, we cursed through sludge,**

These images are very direct and unpleasant and immediately show that Owen does not believe the sentiment expressed in the title of his poem. During the war, people wanted to imagine brave, healthy soldiers fighting for their country. Owen shows that, although they may have joined the army in that state, the war has damaged them beyond repair.

Brooke's poem is simpler and less densely packed with imagery. However, he does use **personification** to represent England as a woman.

A dust whom England bore. . .
Gave, once, her flowers to love. . .

Why do you think Brooke used this form of imagery?

Structure

The **first poem** has a regular **rhythm and rhyme** scheme. It keeps the poem moving forward. It is divided into four stanzas. The third stanza is only two lines in length, which makes it stand out and gives the lines more impact. This is effective because in these lines Owen explains how he is constantly haunted by the image of another soldier's death.

The punctuation and sentence structure in the poem are used to create a variety of effects.

GAS! GAS! Quick, boys! – An ecstasy of fumbling

The exclamation marks show strong feeling – in this case, terror. They also help to recreate the reality and urgency of somebody shouting.

The **second poem** is written following many of the conventions of a **sonnet**. It is fourteen lines long with ten syllables in each line.

The English sonnet is a **traditional** form made popular by William Shakespeare. The values in this poem are also very traditional, so it makes sense to use the sonnet form.

The sonnet is most often connected to the theme of **love**. Although this poem is about war, one of the central themes is the love of, and willingness to die for, England.

Key Point

Conventions of a traditional sonnet: 14 lines; ten syllables in each line; rhyme scheme – abab cdcd efef gg; subject matter – often love.

Your response

Although it is possible to learn how to identify images and structural features, there is no substitute for a **personal response** to poetry.

- How do these poems make you **feel**?
- Which one did you **prefer**?
- Which poem was easiest to **connect** with?
- What do you think particular **images mean**?

Progress Check

1. What emotion does Owen feel towards the person he addresses as *my friend* in the poem?
2. Who are the *children ardent for some desperate glory*?
3. What is the rhyme scheme of 'The Soldier'?

1 Anger 2 Young boys waiting to sign up to join the war. 3 abab cdcd efefg

Assessment questions

The following questions will help you to prepare for the Optional Tests **or** APP tasks.

Read the poem below.

'Hide and Seek' *by Vernon Scannell*

Yoohoo! I'm ready! Come and find me!
The sacks in the toolshed smell like the seaside.
You make yourself little in the salty dark,
Close your eyes tight and hope your feet aren't showing.
Better not risk another call, they might be close.   5
Don't sneeze whatever happens. The floor is cold.
They're probably searching the bushes near the swing.
What's that? That sounds like them. They're coming in!
Don't breathe or move. Still. Someone knocks a can.
Feet mutter. Somebody comes very close,   10
A scuffle of words, a laugh, and then they're gone.
They might be back. Careful in case they come.
They'll try the greenhouse, then in here again.
They're taking a long time, but they'll come back.
Risk a peep out, perhaps? Not yet; they might creep in.   15
A good hiding-place, this: the best you've ever found.
It's funny though, they haven't tried again.
Can't hear a thing. They must be miles away.
The dark damp smell of sand is thicker now.
Give them another call: *Yoo-hoo! Come and find me!*   20
But they are still elsewhere. They'll think you're clever,
And ask you where you hid. Don't tell them. Keep it secret.
It's cold in here. You can't hear anything.
But wait. Let them hunt a little longer;
Think of them frowning at each other   25
Where can he be? We've looked all over.
Something tickles on your nose. Your legs are stiff.
Just a little longer and then creep out.
They're not coming back. You've tricked them properly.
All right. Push off the sacks. That's better.   30
Good to be rid of that unpleasant smell.
Out of the shed. *Hey! Here I am! I'm here!*
I've won the game! You couldn't find me!
The darkening garden watches. Nothing stirs.
The bushes hold their breath. The air is cold.   35
Yes, here you are, but where are they who sought you?

---

1. Explain what happens in this poem. **(AF2)**
2. Read lines 29–36 again and think about what happens earlier in the poem.
   How does the boy feel about being alone? **(AF3)**
3. Comment on the effectiveness of the punctuation in lines 8–10. **(AF5)**

Assessment questions

'Nettles' *by Vernon Scannell*

My son aged three fell in the nettle bed.
'Bed' seemed a curious name for those green spears,
That regiment of spite behind the shed:
It was no place for rest. With sobs and tears
The boy came seeking comfort and I saw
White blisters beaded on his tender skin.
We soothed him till his pain was not so raw.
At last he offered us a watery grin,
And then I took my billhook, honed the blade
And went outside and slashed in fury with it
Till not a nettle in that fierce parade
Stood upright any more. And then I lit
A funeral pyre to burn the fallen dead,
But in two weeks the busy sun and rain
Had called up tall recruits behind the shed:
My son would often feel sharp wounds again.

How does the poet recreate the scene in this poem?

Think about:
- the way actions are described
- the structure, imagery and vocabulary used in the poem. **(AF5 + 6)**

4 Reading non-fiction

After studying this section you should be able to:

- understand an autobiography text
- understand travel writing
- identify key points in leaflets
- read advertisements with understanding
- compare the content of different newspapers
- read for information and research

To achieve the following National Curriculum levels you need to do the following for each level.

Level 4

- Find **information** and **ideas** in a text.
- Explain **your views** of a text.
- Be aware of the **purpose** of the text.

Level 5

- Identify **key features**, **themes** and **characters** in a text.
- **Select sentences, phrases** and **relevant information** to support your views.
- **Collect** and **collate** information from different sources.

Level 6

- Identify different **layers of meaning**.
- Comment on the **significance** and **effect of different devices**, including layout where appropriate.
- **Summarise** a range of information from **different sources**.

Level 7

- Show **understanding** of the way information is conveyed in a range of texts.
- **Select** and **analyse** information and ideas.
- Give a **personal response** to the text.

4.1 Reading autobiography

Literary non-fiction

Writers of **autobiography**, **biography** and **travel writing** use many of the same devices and techniques as fiction writers because, although these texts are based on fact, the main purpose is to entertain.

Recount

Autobiography follows the main conventions of this non-fiction style: events are retold in **chronological order**; it is written in the **past tense** using time connectives; it focuses on identified groups of people.

An **autobiography** is a personal life story. The author selects and reconstructs events from their own life to share with the public. A personal account may be **biased**, and may leave out some details whilst emphasising others for effect. The following extract from Laurie Lee's autobiography, *Cider with Rosie*, recounts one of his earliest memories. As you read it, think about the techniques he uses to bring his account to life.

Key Point	Bias – if a piece of writing is biased, it takes a particular point of view; unbiased writing is balanced and takes account of both sides of an argument.

Emotive language

Extended metaphor

Repetition

Simile

Simile

Simile

I was set down from the carrier's cart at the age of three; and there with a sense of **bewilderment and terror** my life in the village began.

The June grass, amongst which I stood, was taller than I was, and I wept. I had never been so close to grass before. It **towered** above me and all around me, each blade tattooed with tiger-skins of sunlight. It was knife-edged, **dark and a wicked green, thick as a forest** and alive with grasshoppers that chirped and chattered and **leapt through the air like monkeys.**

I was lost and didn't know where to move. A tropic heat oozed up from the ground, rank with sharp odours of roots and nettles. **Snow-clouds** of elder-blossom banked in the sky, **showering** upon me the fumes and **flakes** of their sweet and giddy suffocation. High overhead ran **frenzied** larks, **screaming, as though the sky were tearing apart**.

For the first time in my life I was out of the sight of humans. For the **first time in my life** I was alone in a world whose behaviour I could neither predict nor fathom: a world of birds that squealed, of plants that stank, of insects that sprang about without warning. I was lost and I did not expect to be found again. I put back my head and howled, and the sun hit me smartly on the face, **like a bully**.

From this daylight nightmare I was wakened, as from many another, by the appearance of my sisters. They came scrambling and calling up the steep rough bank, and parting the long grass found me. Faces of rose, familiar, living; huge shining faces **hung up like shields** between me and the sky; faces with grins and white teeth (some broken) to be **conjured up like genii** with a howl, brushing off terror with their broad scoldings and affection. They leaned over me – one, two, three – their mouths smeared with red currants and their hands dripping with juice.

"There, there, it's all right, don't you wail any more. Come down 'ome and we'll stuff you with currants."

From *Cider With Rosie* by Laurie Lee

Word level

Autobiography is from the Greek words: **autos** – self, **bios** – life and **graphein** – to write. An autobiography is a 'self-written life story'.

To learn the spelling of this word, split it into the three parts and learn to spell each section: **Auto bio graphy**. This method will help you to learn lots of other words too, such as **autograph**, **biology**, **photograph**.

Progress Check

Read the extract on page 57 then answer these questions.

1. Which two words in the first sentence show how the boy feels?
2. Why is the boy frightened?
3. How many sentences in the second paragraph are complex sentences?
4. Which phrase is repeated to show that the boy is experiencing something unfamiliar?
5. Find an example of a simile used to describe his sisters.

1 bewilderment and terror 2 He can't see any people and is lost. 3 Three 4 For the first time in my life. . . 5 Like shields. . . like genii. . .

Understanding an autobiography text

AF5
You should be able to:
- comment on how writers convey **setting**, **character** and **mood** through **word choice** and sentence structure;
- recognise how writers' **language choices** can **enhance meaning**.

To show your understanding of the way an author writes and the choices he or she makes, you should be able to write about a range of features in the text.

Setting and mood

The way the setting is described helps to convey the **mood** of this piece of writing. Laurie Lee is writing about the first time he saw a place and he found the experience very frightening. The language he uses emphasises his fear.

Key Point

Setting – where the action takes place.
Mood – the way a piece of writing makes you feel or the way the characters in the text feel.

Emotive vocabulary

- In the first sentence, the words *bewilderment* and *terror* are used to set a mood of fear and confusion.
- The word *towered*, used to describe the tall grass, is a powerful word that makes the grass seem threatening. He also describes the grass as being *a wicked green*.
- He uses the words *frenzied* and *screaming* to describe the larks. This makes the situation sound dangerous. If he wanted to create a happy mood he might have used the words *excited* and *singing*.
- The phrase a *tropic heat oozed* makes you think of a jungle or a rain forest.

Key Point	Emotive vocabulary – words and phrases that make the reader respond emotionally.

Figurative language

Similes

The author uses this device to make an English meadow seem like a dangerous and unfamiliar jungle. An adult reader might not be able to imagine being frightened in a field, but the similes help to create an unfamiliar setting – being lost in a jungle would frighten most people! The grass is described as being *as thick as a forest* and the grasshoppers are *like monkeys*.

The author also uses similes to change familiar symbols. The sun is usually connected with pleasant feelings. However, because he is so frightened even the sun becomes dangerous: *the sun hit me smartly on the face, like a bully*.

Metaphors

The grass is described as being *tattooed with tiger skins of sunlight*. This image links to the jungle idea, but it also gives the reader a sense of how close the grass was because the description is so detailed.

AF5
This is an **extended metaphor**.

The elder-blossom is described in terms of the weather. The author uses the words *snow-clouds*, *showering* and *flakes* to describe the flowers. He uses this description because the blossom is white and it is blown across the sky in clouds. It also adds to the confusion he feels – it is a hot, summer day but he uses the imagery of winter.

Characters

In the final paragraphs the author introduces his sisters, and this changes the mood of the text.

Key Point	Characters – the people who feature in fiction and literary non-fiction.

Description

Things have been described as unfamiliar, but his sisters are safe and familiar; they are very real: *white teeth (some broken)*; *broad scoldings and affection; their mouths smeared with red currants*.

Their voices are brought to life with the representation of their accent and dialect: *"come down 'ome and we'll stuff you with currants."*

Sentence structure

Throughout this extract there is a variety of sentence structures. This makes the writing more interesting and lively.

In the fourth paragraph, the opening two sentences begin in exactly the same way: *For the first time in my life*. This repetition emphasises the fact that he faces an unfamiliar situation.

<table>
<tr><td>**Key Point**</td><td>**Sentence structure** – this is the way sentences are put together. See Chapter 11 for simple, compound and complex sentences.</td></tr>
</table>

The second sentence is a **complex sentence**, which contrasts with the **simple sentences** surrounding it.

After the colon in the complex sentence there is a list of the dangers he faces (notice the use of commas). The **punctuation** within the sentence helps to create a sense of the problems mounting up.

The sentence that follows is a compound sentence, giving equal weight to both clauses. This allows the author to make his opinion sound like a statement of fact, making it more powerful: *I was lost and did not expect to be found again*.

> ### Word level
>
> **Genii** is the plural form of **genie**. Other words that form their plural in this way end in **-us** and have Latin roots.
>
> **Rule:** to form the plural replace the **-us** with **-i**.
>
> **Examples:** cactus → cacti, radius → radii
>
> **Have a go:** What are the plurals of **fungus**, **locus** and **genius**?

Progress Check

1. The cues to start a new paragraph are: **time**, **topic** or **talk**. What is the most common reason for a change of paragraph in the extract from *Cider with Rosie*? TIME / TOPIC / TALK
2. Is the particular way you pronounce words known as your **accent** or your **dialect**?
3. A compound sentence has more than one clause. TRUE or FALSE?
4. A simile is a comparison of two objects using the words *like* or *as*. TRUE or FALSE?
5. A topic sentence appears at the beginning / middle / end of a paragraph.

1 Topic   2 Accent   3 True   4 True   5 Beginning

4.2 Reading travel writing

What is travel writing?

Travel writing is another form of **recount** and is very similar to **autobiography** You need to look out for the same features and textual conventions when reading travel writing as you do when reading autobiography.

In travel writing, places and the people who live there are emphasized.

Read the following extract and think about what kind of impression you are given about the place that is described and the people who live there.

Rhetorical question	And so I went to Edinburgh. **Can there anywhere be a more beautiful and beguiling city to arrive at by train early on a crisp, dark Novembery evening?** To emerge from the bustling, **subterranean bowels** of Waverley Station and find yourself in the very heart of such a glorious city is a happy experience indeed. I hadn't been to Edinburgh for years and had forgotten just how **captivating** it can be. Every monument was lit with golden floodlights – the castle and Bank of Scotland headquarters on the hill, the Balmoral Hotel and the Scott Memorial down below – which gave them a certain **eerie grandeur**. The city was abustle with end-of-day activity. Buses swept through Princes Street and shop and office workers **scurried** along the pavements, **hastening** home to have their haggis and **cock-a-leekie** soup and indulge in a few **skirls** or whatever it is Scots do when the sun goes **doon**.

Labels around extract: Rhetorical question, Emotive vocabulary, Verb choices, Emotive vocabulary, Personification, Sense of difference, Long complex sentence, Metaphor

I'd booked a room in the Caledonian Hotel, which was a rash and **extravagant** thing to do, but it's a **terrific** building and an Edinburgh institution and I just had to be part of it for one night, so I set off for it down Princes Street, past the **Gothic rocket ship** of the Scott Memorial, unexpectedly **exhilarated** to find myself among the hurrying throngs and the sight of the castle on its craggy mount outlined against a pale evening sky.

From *Notes from a Small Island* by Bill Bryson

Key Point — **Rhetorical question** – a question that does not require an answer. Rhetorical questions are used for emphasis or to create particular effects.

Word level

Doon – Scottish pronunciation of the word **down**.

Skirl – the shrill sound made by bagpipes.

Bill Bryson includes these words to give a sense of the place he is writing about.

Understanding a piece of travel writing

People

The **people** are not described in any detail in this passage. The writer creates the impression that they are busy, a little distant and different to people he has encountered in other parts of Britain.

Place

The writer creates a **romantic picture** of a beautiful but very busy city. He gives the impression that, like the people who live there, Edinburgh is somehow alien and different to other places he has visited.

Vocabulary choices

- **Emotive vocabulary** – the writer uses words like *beautiful*, *beguiling* and *captivating* to suggest that he has fallen in love with the city. The phrase *eerie grandeur* makes the city seem imposing and slightly frightening.
- **Verb choices** – the writer chooses the verbs *swept*, *scurried*, *hastening* and *hurrying* to describe the movement of people and objects in Edinburgh. This gives the impression that everybody is busy and things move very quickly. It makes the place seem lively.

Figurative language and language devices

- **Alliteration** – in the opening sentences of the passage the writer creates patterns by using alliteration – *beautiful and beguiling city. . . the bustling subterranean bowels of Waverley Station*. The description of the city is quite poetic and romantic; the use of alliteration enhances this.
- **Personification** – if Edinburgh is a person, then the underground station represents the *bowels* of the city. The station is dark and dirty; it provides a strong contrast with the beautiful city above the ground. The writer continues the image by referring to the *heart* of the city.
- **Metaphor** – by describing the monument as a *gothic rocket ship*, the writer gives the impression that it has landed there from another planet. This adds to the atmosphere of difference that he has created throughout this passage.

Sentence structure

The opening sentence is a **simple sentence**: a statement of fact, which introduces the topic of the whole passage. The rest of the passage is mostly written in extended **complex** and **compound sentences**.

The second sentence is a **rhetorical question**; it makes the reader more involved and requires them to imagine the place that is being described.

The final sentence is very long. Each **clause** in the sentence is used to build up a sense of excitement and wonderment as the writer explores the city. This sentence also reflects the description of the **hurrying throng**.

Below is another extract from Bill Bryson's book.

I took a train to Liverpool. They were having a festival of litter when I arrived. Citizens had taken time off from their busy activities to add crisp packets, empty cigarette boxes, and carrier-bags to the otherwise bland and neglected landscape. They fluttered gaily in the bushes and brought colour and texture to pavements and gutters. And to think that elsewhere we stick these objects in rubbish bags.

In another bout of extravagant madness, I had booked a room in the Adelphi Hotel. I had seen it from the street on earlier visits and it appeared to have an old-fashioned grandeur about it that I was keen to investigate. On the other hand, it looked expensive and I wasn't sure my trousers could stand another session in the trouser press. So I was most agreeably surprised when I checked in to discover that I was entitled to a special weekend rate and that there would be money spare for a nice meal and a parade of beer in any of the many wonderful pubs in which Liverpool specializes.

And so, soon afterwards, I found myself, like all fresh arrivals in Liverpool, in the grand and splendorous surroundings of the Philharmonic, clutching a pint glass. . .

From *Notes from a Small Island* by Bill Bryson

Progress Check

Answer the following questions about the passage above.
1. What kind of sentence is the first sentence in the passage?
   simple / complex / compound
2. What is the name of the device used in the phrase *splendorous surroundings*?
3. Does the opening description of Liverpool create a positive or negative impression?
4. Does the writer like Liverpool?

1 Simple 2 Alliteration 3 Negative 4 Yes

4.3 Reading leaflets

Text conventions of leaflets

YORKSHIRE MUSEUM, MUSEUM GARDENS, YORK

the Upright Ape

Colourful pictures

MEET YOUR ANCESTORS!
20 July to 16 February
at the
Yorkshire Museum, Museum Gardens, York   YORK

Exclamation

Leaflets follow a range of non-fiction conventions.

- **Information text** – leaflets follow many of the conventions of this non-fiction text style: **purpose**: to give information; **structure**: clearly organised; **language**: present tense, third person.
- **Persuasive text** – leaflets are often intended to persuade as well as inform. The conventions of persuasive texts are: **structure**: statement of argument followed by a range of persuasive points in favour of the argument; **language**: present tense, often in the second person, emotive and persuasive language.
- **Layout** – what a leaflet looks like is very important. Features of layout include: pictures, columns, font size and style.

Look at this leaflet, which is continued on page 64, to see how effective these conventions are.

Imperative verb

Persuasive panel

Directive

The Upright Ape

MEET YOUR ANCESTORS!

Who are we?

Where do we come from?

Find the answers to these questions in our new exhibition 'The Upright Ape'.

Discover your roots with the aid of exciting hands-on displays, stunning life size reconstructions and real fossils.

Walk in the footsteps of an ape, keep watch for deadly leopards and test your strength against a Neanderthal – a truly interactive experience awaits you.

The Upright Ape is a hands-on journey through time which will entertain and intrigue all age groups.

Other exhibitions and events this year

Alcuin and Charlemagne – The Golden Age of York
The story is told through the letters of Alcuin, richly illuminated books, sculptures and precious objects of ivory, crystal, silver and gold.
Until 26 September

W A Ismay Collection
A celebration of the lifelong passion of Bill Ismay, whose spectacular collection of post-war studio pottery was recently bequeathed to the Yorkshire Museum.
From 8 September

Wildlife Photographer of the Year Exhibition
See the winning and highly commended entries from this worldwide competition.
17 November to 26 January

I would like to receive information on events and new exhibitions at the Yorkshire Museum, York Castle Museum and York City Art Gallery.

Name_____

Address_____

_____

Postcode_____

e-mail address_____

I would prefer to receive information by:
e-mail ☐   Post ☐

To be included on the mailing list please return this completed form to: Marketing Department, Yorkshire Museum, Museum Gardens, York, YO1 7FR.

Lots of pictures

Information panel

Written in 2nd person to involve the reader

YORKSHIRE MUSEUM

MUSEUM GARDENS, YORK

Set in 10 acres of botanical gardens in the centre of York, the Yorkshire Museum houses some of the richest archaeological finds in Europe and covers over 1000 years of local history.

Take a journey back through time and discover the Roman, Anglo-Saxon, Viking and Medieval history and treasures of York and Yorkshire. Don't miss the exquisite world-famous Middleham Jewel, a 15th century gold pendant adorned with a magnificent sapphire.

You can also visit the Abbey Gallery and the majestic ruin of the medieval St Mary's Abbey, once one of the most wealthy and powerful abbeys in the north.

Also, meet the Jurassic sea dragons in the Hunters and Hunted Gallery.

Information panel

Persuasive panel

Directive

Map

The Upright Ape

YORKSHIRE MUSEUM, MUSEUM GARDENS, YORK

OPEN DAILY 10am – 5pm

The Yorkshire Museum is situated in the Museum Gardens in the centre of York, just a short walk from York Railway Station. Follow the signs to the city centre. There is a regular Park and Ride service from four sites on main routes as you enter York and there are also two car parks within a short walk of the museum.

ADMISSION

Adults £4.50
Child/Concession £2.95
Family £14.00 (2 adults and up to 3 children)

Group bookings and school parties welcome. Call for details of group rates.

York residents are entitled to free entry to the Yorkshire Museum permanent collections and reduced entry to touring exhibitions, on presentation of a YorkCard.

5 DAY MUSEUM PASS
allowing unlimited entry into Yorkshire Museum, York Castle Museum and York City Art Gallery.
Adult £9.00   Child/Concession £5.00   Family £27.50

All galleries are accessible to wheelchair users and toilet facilities are available to all visitors.
The museum shop has an extensive range of gifts to remind you of your visit.

For further information please contact:

Yorkshire Museum   Tel: (01904) 551800
Museum Gardens   Fax: (01904) 551802
York   e-mail: yorkshire.museum@york.gov.uk
YO1 7FR   www.york.gov.uk

YORK

MARYGATE

YORK CITY ART GALLERY

RIVER OUSE

YORKSHIRE MUSEUM

MUSEUM GARDENS

York Minster

RAILWAY STATION

LENDAL BRIDGE

ROUGIER STREET

LENDAL

HOW TO FIND US

Sentence types

Statements

A **statement** is a sentence that gives information to the reader. This kind of sentence ends with a full stop. These sentences are used in the information sections of the leaflet – in the *Other exhibitions and events. . .* and *OPEN DAILY* panels of the leaflet.

The Yorkshire Museum is situated. . .

All galleries are accessible to wheelchair users. . .

Exclamations

An **exclamation** is usually a short sentence that shows strong feelings.

In this leaflet the exclamation *Meet your ancestors!* is used twice. In this case the exclamation mark indicates surprise. It is linked to the pictures of the 'upright apes' and suggests that human beings are directly related to the apes.

Directives

A **directive** is a sentence that expects someone to do something. If it is a sharp command, the sentence should end with an **exclamation mark** – **Shut up! Sit down!**

This leaflet contains polite instructions that aim to persuade.

Discover your roots with the aid of exciting hands-on displays. . .

Walk in the footsteps of an ape. . .

Commands or instructions use the **imperative** form of the verb – *discover*, *walk*, *find*.

Questions

A **question** is a sentence that asks for information and requires an answer.

In this leaflet the questions are concerned with human origins. They are the kind of 'big questions' that people ask themselves when they are thinking about how they fit into life.

Who are we? Where do we come from?

The leaflet claims that the exhibition has all the answers to these questions.

Progress Check

1. How many exclamations are there in the leaflet?
2. How much does a family museum pass cost?
3. What form of verb is used in this sentence: *Also, meet the Jurassic sea dragons. . . ?*
4. What is the main exhibition called?

1 Two 2 £27.50 3 Imperative 4 The Upright Ape

Word level

Directive sentences nearly always have an **imperative structure**. This means that the verb is used in its basic form, with no endings (-ed, -s, -ing, etc.). The **imperative** form does not contain a **subject**.

Vocabulary choices

This leaflet uses lots of **persuasive** vocabulary, particularly in the inside section: *exciting, stunning, deadly, entertain and intrigue*.

This kind of language makes the display sound appealing and worth visiting.

The information sections also contain persuasive language – *richly illuminated books*.

Layout

- **Pictures** – the pictures are colourful and take up a large proportion of the page. They are intended to show that the apes look similar to human beings.
- **Colour** – the leaflet is very colourful and appealing. The writing is white so that it stands out clearly from the background.
- **Titles** – the titles are larger than the rest of the text. *The Upright Ape* title is in a different font style because it is the main title.
- **Columns and paragraphs** – the text is in columns and short paragraphs, which make it easier to read. The columns make it easier to identify the informative and persuasive sections.
- **Other features** – information about prices and opening times is presented in note form.

Admission
Adults £4.50

AF4
You should be able to analyse the overall structure of a text to identify how key ideas are developed.

To judge the **effectiveness** of this leaflet you should consider all of these points together. Do you think it would be effective in persuading people to visit the exhibition? Would you visit the exhibition after reading this leaflet?

Word level

Prepositions hold sentences together – they are the words that show how one thing is related to another: **to, between, off, on, into, above, beneath**.

Find the answers to these questions. . .

The story is told through the letters of Alcuin. . .

4.4 Reading advertisements

Key Point

Media – newspapers, film, radio, magazines, internet, posters and advertisements are all forms of media.

How an advertisement is put together

When you read an advertisement there are many factors you should consider, including:

- **target audience**
- **brand names**
- **slogans**
- **pictures and colour**
- **special offers / coupons**
- **emotive / persuasive vocabulary**.

Target audience

Advertisers aim particular products at different groups of people according to **age, sex, social class** and **interests**. They will often make assumptions about people and label or stereotype them.

Who do you think these products would be aimed at: nappies, diamonds, mint chocolates, sports cars?

What kind of products would be aimed at these people: teenagers, 25-year-old single men, 40-year-old working mums?

Brand names

Brand names are chosen carefully. They can suggest particular lifestyles, values or interests and are intended to appeal to the target audience.

Nissan Primera: this suggests quality. Primera is similar to premium and premier.

Ford Ka: the spelling of Ka suggests novelty and simplicity. It is modern and futuristic. It is also bound to stick in your mind when you are looking for a new car!

Slogans

A **slogan** has to be catchy and memorable. Slogans use a range of devices: **alliteration, repetition, puns, questions, personal pronouns and humour**.

Have a break. Have a KitKat. (KitKat)   **Repetition**
The totally tropical taste. (Lilt)   **Alliteration**

Pictures and colour

All **pictures** try to make you feel something and most are **biased**, even photographs. They create a view of what the world is like using different tricks such as lighting and colour.

Different colours have different associations that can be linked to particular products.

Yellow: freshness, sunlight, lemons. This colour would be good for advertising washing-up liquid.
Green: countryside, natural, healthy. What would you use this colour for?
What do you associate these colours with: red, black, orange, gold, blue?

Special offers / coupons

Advertisers often appear to offer 'something for nothing': if you buy one product you will receive another one free or half price. These offers are an **incentive** to try a new product or to encourage **loyalty** to an existing one.

Emotive / persuasive vocabulary

In advertising you will find lots of words and phrases that are intended to persuade you or appeal to your emotions.

tempting	silky	free
chocolate	romantic	powerful
creamy	traditional	mouthwatering
luxurious	like mum used to make	

Progress Check

1. Who would these words and phrases appeal to: *look younger, healthy, firmer, smooth, creamy*?
2. What kind of device does this slogan use? *The future's bright. The future's Orange.* (Orange)
3. What is a target audience?

1 Women concerned about the appearance of their skin.   2 Repetition
3 The group of people a product is aimed at.

Analysing an advertisement

In order to assess the effectiveness of an advertisement, you must consider the importance of each element of the factors discussed above.

Study the advert on page 69, and then read about how each element has been used.

- **Target audience** – this advert is aimed at people who have a lot of time and money – the cruise is 35 days and costs nearly £4000. The style of the advert – lots of text, rich colours and continued reference to warmth – suggests that it is aimed at retired couples who like to travel.
- **Picture** – the colours are warm and relaxing and link to those mentioned in the text. The picture is appealing and inviting. It makes the location seem romantic.
- **Slogan** – *Make the world your home.* This slogan suggests home comforts and familiarity in an unfamiliar environment. The cruise is over a month long, so the ship will become the passengers' home, whilst allowing them to experience the world.
- **Special offers** – the *15% off* offer is in bold type to attract attention. It is used to encourage people to book early, as it is only available for a limited time.

Feeling the winter blues? Escape to the magnificent Mediterranean on a 35-day cruise

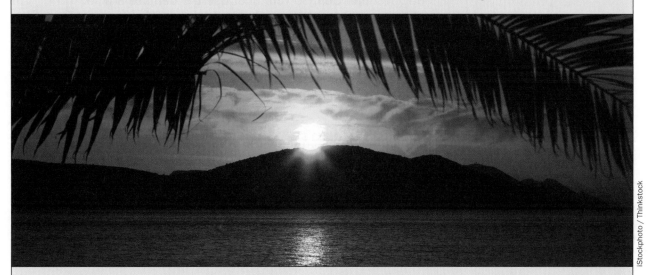

iStockphoto / Thinkstock

Feeling jaded by the dark winter nights, biting winds and constant cold? Prefer to feel the soft caress of the warm sun, swim in cool, sparkling aquamarine sea and stroll around fascinating ancient cities? Then look no further than a delightful 35-day cruise around the sunny Mediterranean.

Our 5-week cruise will take you on a on a never-to-be forgotten tour, with visits to breathtaking Monte Carlo, historic Cadiz, ancient Rome, picturesque Dubrovnik and the spectacular Amalfi coast.

While away warm balmy days on our sumptuous cruise ship, enjoying delicious continental food and fantastic entertainment, whilst experiencing everything the Mediterranean has to offer – rugged mountain vistas, beautiful sandy beaches, fascinating old towns with quaint pavement cafes, castles, museums, famous landmarks and more! Meander down shady cobbled streets, browse around the local shops or enjoy an inviting glass of Pinot Noir with local specialities at a pavement cafe.

History, adventure and glorious scenery await you at every port of call!

Prices start from £3750*.

Book by the end of February and benefit from an extra 15% off! That's a fantastic saving!

Free minibus travel is also available – limited places available.

Departure dates from December 1 to April 24.

Terms and conditions apply.

To book, call
0820 700 923
quoting reference
LLJ/520/Q

Sail Away Cruise Lines
Make the world your home

SMITH & TAYLOR

Conditions: 1. Valid on new telephone bookings to Smith & Taylor. Each operator's booking conditions apply. 2. All cruises are subject to availability. The example savings are correct at time of going to press. 3. Comprehensive cover is required at booking. 4. There will be a charge of £3.50 for all bookings within 5 weeks of departure. 5. This offer is open to residents of the UK aged 18 and over. 6. Prices subject to availability. 7. Prices based on 2 adults sharing an inside twin cabin and includes taxes.

- **Emotive / persuasive vocabulary** – the main copy is full of emotive and persuasive vocabulary: *swim in cool, sparkling aquamarine sea and stroll around fascinating ancient cities*.

The language is intended to make the reader feel relaxed and it emphasises the beauty, history and romantic nature of the cruise. The language is very descriptive, which helps to emphasise the enjoyment of discovery and adventure.

Word level

Articles are like **prepositions**: sentences don't make sense without them. An **article** is a **determiner** that introduces a **noun** or **noun phrase** (see **Chapter 11**).

- Definite article: **the**.
  around the Mediterranean Sea – there is only one Mediterranean Sea, so you must use the **definite** article
- Indefinite article: **a** or **an**.
  (Use **an** when the word that follows begins with a **vowel** – a, e, i, o, u.)
  or enjoy an inviting glass of. . .

Progress Check

1. What kind of information does the small print contain?
2. *Departure dates from December 1 to April 24. Prices start from £3750.* FACT or OPINION?
3. Is there more fact or more opinion in this advertisement?
4. Which season will the cruise help you to avoid?

1 Terms and conditions   2 Fact   3 Opinion   4 Winter

4.5 Reading newspapers

Key Point

Broadsheet – a newspaper considered to be more factual and serious in tone than a tabloid newspaper. Aims to **inform** rather than entertain. Examples: *The Guardian*, *The Times*.
Tabloid – aims to **inform and entertain**. A tabloid paper is more likely to use emotive language and sensationalise stories. Pictures and headlines are far more important in a tabloid. Examples: *The Sun*, *The Mirror*.

If you **compare** two newspaper articles from different newspaper formats, you will notice **differences** in many of the areas discussed below.

Analysing a newspaper story

When you are studying a newspaper report, you should think about the following.
- **Layout**
  - How is the article broken up?
  - Is the headline effective? How much of the page does it take up? Does it use any language devices?
  - Where does the story appear in the newspaper?
  - What use is made of pictures, captions and sub-headings?
- **Audience**
  - Who is it aimed at?
  - Consider: age, class, occupation, interests.

AF6
You should be able to compare the presentation of ideas, values or emotions in related or contrasting texts.

- **Language**
  - What kind of words are used – simple, complex / polysyllabic?
  - Consider the length of sentences and sentence construction.
  - Think about the use of jargon.
  - Is emotive language used?
- **Tone** – Is the article informative, shocking, humorous or sad?
- **Bias**
  - Is the article balanced or does it take sides?
  - Does the whole newspaper have a political bias?
- **Interviews** – Who has been interviewed and why?
- **Personal response** – How do you respond to this kind of reporting?

4.6 Reading for information and research

AF2
You should be able to use appropriate reading strategies to extract particular information, e.g. highlighting, scanning.

When you read for **information**, you may use a range of reading techniques, depending on what you are reading and why you are reading it. There are three main types of reading: **scanning**, **skimming** and **intensive reading**.

Key Point	There are three kinds of reading for information: **scanning**, **skimming** and **intensive reading**.

Scanning

When you want to find a particular piece of information in a text, you may **scan read** for a **key word or phrase**. For example, if you want to know what time your favourite television programme is on, you don't need to read the TV listings magazine from cover to cover. Instead, you find the correct page for that day's television and scan the columns until you find the name of your television programme.

Use scanning to:
- **read timetables**
- find **keys words** and page references in an index
- find a **spelling** in a **dictionary**
- find a **number** in a **telephone directory**
- find the **relevant section** in a **leaflet**.

Once you have scanned a text, you may decide you need to read part of it more closely, e.g. the definition of the word you were looking for in the dictionary, or a summary of your favourite television programme.

Skimming

Skimming is a technique that allows you to read a whole text quickly, which can be very useful in exams. Skimming involves reading the whole text quickly to get a general understanding of what it is about and pick out key words and phrases.

- **For general reading and research** – this technique will help you to decide whether a text has the information you are looking for. You may then decide to read all or part of the text paying closer attention to detail.
- **In an exam** – the text will definitely be relevant to the task you have been set. This reading technique will help you to identify the important sections that you will need to read more closely. Once you have skimmed the text, read the questions carefully. Then you will be able to **skim** and **scan** for the key words and sections you need to answer each question.

AF2
You should be able to appraise the value and relevance of information found and acknowledge sources.

Intensive reading

Once you have identified the fact that a text has the information you require, you need to read the relevant sections more carefully. **Intensive reading** allows you to gain the maximum information from a text. For general reading and research you should:

- read more **slowly**
- **check** definitions of words you don't understand
- **re-read** sentences or groups of sentences that express complex ideas
- make decisions about exactly what is **relevant** to your research
- **make notes or answer questions** based on the information you have learned – **don't copy from the text** unless you are quoting an example or you have been explicitly instructed to copy.

In an exam you should try to follow the same guidelines. However, you will have a time limit and you may not be allowed to check definitions – **you are not allowed to take dictionaries into many exams**.

Progress Check

1. What kind of reading technique would you use to find a place on a map or in an atlas? scanning / skimming / intensive reading
2. Skim reading can completely replace intensive reading in an exam. TRUE or FALSE?
3. When you make notes you should always copy directly from the text you have read. TRUE or FALSE?

1 Scanning 2 False 3 False

Assessment questions

The following questions will help you to prepare for the Optional Tests or APP tasks.

You can check their progress by logging onto their blog at www.sistersstatesprint159-637-T8ghp3.co.uk

Digital Vision / Thinkstock

Dynamic Duo's Dash Across the States

By Charlie Williams

Two intrepid runners from West Yorkshire have almost completed their daring run across America in order to raise awareness for their favourite charity, the Primrose Trust.

Charlotte Johnson (29) and her sister Caroline Smith (27), who both attended Raventop Grammar School, started their incredible journey in Seattle in Washington State and are running all the way across America to finish in Miami, Florida. This incredible journey of more than 2700 miles (4400km) has seen them running through over 10 different states, including Idaho, Colorado, Kansas, Arkansas and Georgia.

The plucky pair is attempting to complete their epic run in record time and are on track to complete the run in the next 3 weeks.

Their incredible feat has not been without its risks. As well as the many injuries they have picked up, the adventurous duo were mugged shortly after entering Georgia, and they witnessed a gun battle between police and armed robbers on their way through Kansas.

1. How old is Caroline Smith? **(AF2)**
2. Which paragraph gives details about the dangers of their journey? **(AF2)**
3. Name two layout features used in this newspaper article. **(AF4)**
4. Which sentence is the topic sentence? **(AF4)**
5. Explain why the word 'epic' has been used. **(AF5)**

Assessment questions

Read the National Railway Museum leaflet below and look closely at the layout of the leaflet.

How does the writer of this leaflet try to inform people and persuade them to visit the museum?

Think about:
- the content of the leaflet
- particular words and phrases that are used
- layout **(AF4 and AF5)**

Looking for a fun-packed, family day out, where entry is free for the under 17s and over 60s? Then why not come along to the National Railway Museum in York? It's the largest railway museum in the world!

Here, you'll experience the incredible story of the train as you've never seen or heard it before. You'll be amazed at how much we have to offer for a truly memorable journey through the past and into the present.

Rocket to Eurostar

See our replica of Stephenson's *Rocket*, the 172 year old engine responsible for reshaping the future of the steam locomotive. And the world record-breaking *Mallard* - its amazing steam speed record of 126 mph still stands

to this day. Contrast this with the sleek, streamlined shape of *Eurostar*. Its futuristic design reflects the state-of-the-art journey it makes every day, deep beneath the Channel. Or catch the technologically advanced Japanese Bullet train *Shinkansen*, as it goes on permanent display from 14 July.

Royal Coaches and Exhibitions

With the finest collection of Royal coaches in the world, dating back to before the Victorian era, you'll be amazed at how monarchs travelled in our *Palaces on Wheels* exhibition. And see how we deliver the story of the mail in *Moving Things - The Mail* via touch-screen technology, a karaoke machine and a push-button quiz.

5 Plan, draft and present

After studying this section you should be able to:

- plan a piece of writing
- draft and redraft a piece of writing
- present a piece of non-fiction writing

5.1 Planning

Brainstorming

Brainstorming is a good way to start any piece of writing.

- Write down as many ideas, **key words** and feelings as you can about the subject you need to write about.
- As soon as you have an idea, write it down.
- Don't worry about your handwriting or presentation.
- Use the best ideas in your final piece of writing.

Go for five

This technique will help you with descriptive or narrative writing. Try to think of **five** words or phrases for each pre-decided category. For example: **describing a scary forest**.

- **Sounds**: crunching, twigs snapping, shuffling, animals howling. . .
- **Textures**: crumbly moss, rough bark, sharp scratching thorns, ghostly cobwebs brushing my face. . .
- **Sights**: eerie shadows, shapes moving in the darkness, branches like hands reaching out to grab me, pin points of light like eyes. . .

Spider diagrams and brain maps

You could use a **spider diagram** to **brainstorm** your ideas about a character, storyline, memory, event or issue.

Write the central idea or issue in the centre of your page and then branch out from the centre like spider legs with the rest of your ideas. For example, use a spider diagram to brainstorm both sides of an argument about whether schools should have uniform. An example of this is shown on page 76.

A **brain map** is similar to a **spider diagram**, but it allows you to organise your thoughts more clearly by putting in **extra layers**. If you were making a brain map to explore the different aspects of a character in a novel, you might present it like this:

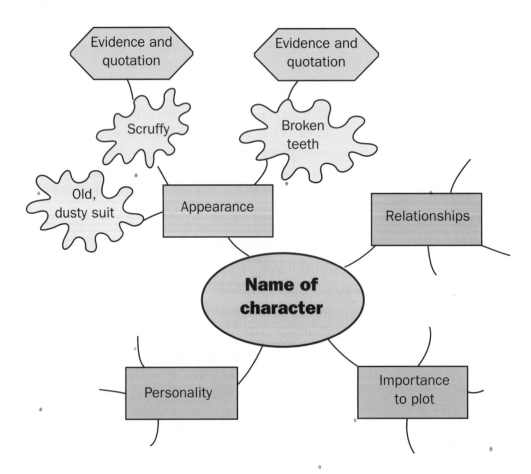

Making notes in a table or chart

Look back at the spider diagram about school uniform. As this brainstorm is looking at two sides of an argument, it may have been more usefully presented in a table.

School uniform	
For	**Against**
Sense of school identity Smart Easy to identify on trips and visits Saves other clothes from wear and tear and subject-related damage, e.g. art, science	Uncomfortable Expensive Unfashionable Impractical for some subjects

Key Point

As you work through the writing chapters you will find more advice about planning and examples of planning formats.

Formal planning

Before beginning an extended piece of writing, it is helpful to make a formal **paragraph plan**.

- **Non-fiction**: decide on the topic of each paragraph and write several bullet points to cover in each one.
- **Fiction**: decide how your story will develop and write several bullet points to show how each section of the plot will unfold.

5.2 Drafting and redrafting

Most major pieces of writing you do at school will be **drafted** and **redrafted**. This means you have a chance to refine and improve your ideas and the way you express them.

First draft

When writing your first draft, follow these guidelines:
- **Follow your plan**.
- **Concentrate** and try to write quite **quickly** in order to get into the rhythm of your writing.
- If you are unhappy with a word or phrase that you've used, **underline** it so that you can come back to it when you **redraft**.

Redrafting

If you are asked to **redraft** a piece of writing this doesn't mean you should copy it out in your best handwriting, although **neatness and legibility** are important. There are many things to look out for when you are redrafting.

Openings

It is important to grab the reader's interest straightaway. In an exam, you need to make sure the examiner can tell immediately that you understand what you've been asked to do. Think about changing **vocabulary or sentence structure** to make the opening more powerful.

Main Content

- Ensure that you have used a **range of sentence structures** in your writing to **vary the pace and create rhythms**.
- Ensure that you have made some **original** and **adventurous vocabulary** choices.
- Ensure that any **imagery is creative** and **original**.
- Check that you have **backed up your opinions** with **evidence and / or quotations**.

Proof reading

Proof reading is the process of re-reading a piece of writing to check the technical accuracy of your writing.

Spelling

- **Check** for any words you may have **misspelt** because you were writing in a hurry.
- **Check** words that you sometimes find confusing, e.g. **common homophones: there, their, they're**.
- **Underline** any words that you are unsure of and use a dictionary to check your spelling.

Remember, you can't use a dictionary in exams.

Punctuation

- Make sure you have used **capital letters** where they are needed.
- Check your use of **apostrophes**.
- Check punctuation in **complex sentences**.
- Read your work out loud to makes sure that your **punctuation helps the sense** of your writing.

Paragraphing

Remember that paragraphs are organised by **time**, **topic** or **talk**. Read through your work and make sure that your ideas are correctly organised into paragraphs.

Key Point	In an exam situation you don't have time for redrafting, but you should always make time for **proof reading**.

5.3 Presentation

The presentation of your final draft is very important. If your work is attractively presented, it will impress your teacher or examiner and give you a sense of pride in your own achievement.

Handwriting

Legible handwriting is important in school and in later life. It ensures that your meaning is expressed clearly and is easily understood. Neat and legible handwriting will encourage the reader to pay closer attention to what you have written.

Typing and word processing

Lots of students have access to computers to produce homework and extended written assignments. Although not compulsory, this helps to ensure that presentation is attractive and legible. If you do use a computer to present your work, think about the following points.

- Make sure that the **font style** and **size** is legible and appropriate to the task.
- Make use of facilities such as **bold type**, **underlining** and **bullet points**, but don't overdo these.
- Don't feel obliged to use all the presentational devices available with the software you are using, e.g. cartoon clip art isn't appropriate in a formal essay or letter.

Key Point	As you will have to write exam answers by hand, **take time to practise writing at speed** to make sure that your handwriting remains legible.

Presenting non-fiction texts

If you are asked to write a non-fiction text that uses different presentational devices, such as **columns, pictures, bullet points** and **different font sizes**, try to use these devices in your own writing.

If you are writing this kind of text in an exam, **don't waste time** with unnecessary **presentation**. For example, if you are writing a leaflet and want to include pictures, don't spend time drawing and colouring in. Instead, draw a box on the page where you would place a picture and write what the picture would show inside.

6 Writing to imagine, explore, entertain

After studying this section you should be able to:

- create believable characters when writing stories and poems
- create realistic and atmospheric settings for stories and poems
- use dialogue to create atmosphere and develop characters
- give your stories and poems a suitable structure
- structure your narrative and experiment with different narrative perspectives.

To achieve the following National Curriculum levels you need to do the following for each level.

Level 4
- Think of an **interesting storyline**.
- **Organise your ideas** to hold the interest of the reader.

Level 5
- Experiment with **figurative language**.
- Create **believable characters**.
- Use **language** and **structure** to create atmosphere.
- Organise writing into paragraphs and make clear links between them.

Level 6
- Maintain a balance of **plot, description** and **dialogue**.
- Vary the pace by using a **range of sentence structures**.
- Control and sequence your writing.

Level 7
- **Sustain** and **develop characters** and **settings** in narrative.
- Experiment with and control a **range of narrative styles**.
- Shape and craft paragraphs for imaginative effect.

6.1 Writing poetry

Personification

AF1
You should be able to make links between your reading of fiction, plays and poetry and the choices you make as a writer.

Re-read the poem 'City Jungle' on page 41. To write a similar poem using **personification**, follow these instructions.

Plan

Think of a place: **the beach**.
Think of six **nouns** you would find at that place:

- sand dunes
- deck chairs
- clouds
- ice cream
- waves
- beach ball.

Think of six **verbs** you would associate with human beings:
Match up the **nouns and verbs**:

sand dunes	giggle
deck chairs	laugh
clouds	dance
ice creams	skip
waves	whisper
beach balls	relax

Key Point

Alliteration – the repetition of a letter or letter sound at the beginning of a sequence of words.
Noun phrase – a group of words with a noun as the central component.

Write

- Think about the best order in which to present these ideas and images.
- Add **adjectives** and **adverbs** to each phrase to create **extended noun phrases**.
- Try to use other devices such as **alliteration** in your poem.

> Brightly coloured bouncing beach balls dance along the shore.
> Fluffy white clouds skip lightly across the sky.
> Sparkling white-tipped waves whisper their secrets to chattering sea shells.
> Stripy deck chairs laugh at giggling, dripping ice creams.
> Sand dunes relax in the sun.

Redraft

- Think about the **shape** of your poem.
- Make decisions about **rhyme and rhythm**.
- Change or add **vocabulary**.

> Brightly coloured bouncing beach balls
> dance along the shore.
> Fluffy white **candyfloss** clouds
> skip lightly across the sky.
> Sparkling ~~white~~ **silver**-tipped waves
> whisper their secrets to chattering sea shells.
> Stripy deck chairs laugh at giggling, dripping ice creams.
> Sand dunes ~~relax~~ **blush** in the **setting** sun

- This poem doesn't have a regular rhyme scheme or rhythm – the personification that runs through the poem acts like the 'glue' which holds it together.
- The shape of the poem is supposed to be like the waves lapping on the shore.

6.2 Creating characters

If you are to create believable characters, you need to know them really well before you start writing. One way to get to know your characters is to create a **fact file**.

Fact file

Name:	Jamie Monks
Age:	15
Occupation:	student at local comprehensive, on the verge of exclusion
Appearance:	short brown hair, faded highlights; blue eyes, angry stare; school uniform always untidy, wears trainers even though it's against the rules; wears baggy skate clothes outside school
Personality:	appears to be a trouble maker and rule breaker; rebellious; teachers think he's disrespectful; good sense of humour, always making friends laugh; low self-esteem, doesn't think he can do or achieve anything; very kind to younger sister
Leisure/hobbies:	everything to do with skateboarding; listening to music (too loud!); being with friends
Ambition:	to win a major skateboarding competition
Fears:	failure – often refuses to attempt new things to avoid failure; turning out like his dad
Family:	lives with mum and younger sister, Allie; dad has left the home – mum always complains that Jamie is just like his dad but never explains what she means
Past / secret:	trying to find his dad, doesn't want mum to know as it will upset her

Character description

What kind of character fact file do you think this person would have?

> Mr Sugden was passing slowly across one end of the room, looking down the corridors and counting the boys as they changed. He was wearing a violet tracksuit. The top was embellished with cloth badges depicting numerous crests and qualifications, and on the breast a white athlete carried the Olympic torch. The legs were tucked into new white football socks, neatly folded at his ankles, and his football boots were polished as black and shiny as the bombs used by assassins in comic strips. The laces binding them had been scrubbed white, and both boots had been fastened identically: two loops of the foot and one of the ankle, and tied in a neat bow under the tab at the back.
>
> From *A Kestrel for a Knave* by Barry Hines

AF1
You should be able to portray characters, directly and indirectly, through description, dialogue and action.

Does this description of Mr Sugden help you to understand the way he behaves in the extract on pages 22–23, and why he dislikes Billy?

Key Point

It isn't possible or desirable to reveal everything about a character through **explicit description** – some of the information about the character should be **implied**. Give your reader clues about characters from the way they behave, what they say and how they say it.

There are more examples of character descriptions in **Chapter 2 Reading fiction and plays**.

Word level

Try to experiment with figurative language. In the description of Mr Sugden, the writer uses a simile: *his football boots were polished as black and shiny as the bombs used by assassins in comic strips*. This links Mr Sugden to danger, but it also gives the impression that the author finds the character a bit foolish and comical.

Key Point

Once you have made a character fact file, you should keep it as a reference to make sure that your character behaves in a believable way throughout the story.

Progress Check

1. You should reveal everything about a character directly. TRUE or FALSE?
2. Mr Sugden doesn't care about his appearance. TRUE or FALSE?
3. The image used to describe Mr Sugden's football boots is a simile / metaphor.

1 False 2 False 3 Simile

Have a go

1. Write a character fact file of your own.
2. Write a short description of that character.
3. Write a short passage about your character, involving action and dialogue to give clues and implied character information to the reader.

6.3 Creating a setting

Creating real places

When you are writing a story, **realistic locations** are just as important as believable characters.

A few miles south of Soledad, the Salinas River drops in close to the hill-side bank and runs deep and green. The water is warm too, for it has slipped twinkling over the yellow sands in the sunlight before reaching the narrow pool. On one side of the river the golden foothill slopes curve up to the strong and rocky Gabilan mountains, but on the valley side the water is lined with trees – willows fresh and green with every spring, carrying in their lower leaf junctures the debris of the winter's flooding; and sycamores with mottled, white, recumbent limbs and branches that arch over the pool. On the sandy bank under the trees the leaves lie deep and so crisp that a lizard makes a great skittering if he runs among them. Rabbits come out of the brush to sit on the sand in the evening, and the damp flats are covered with the night tracks of 'coons, and with the spread pads of dogs from the ranches, and with the split-wedge tracks of deer that come to drink in the dark.

From *Of Mice and Men* by John Steinbeck

In **science fiction** and **fantasy** stories, locations still have to be believable settings for the action taking place there.

That had only taken it as far as the general bay engineering space, the biggest single volume in the ship with the divisions down; nine thousand metres deep, nearly twice that across and filled with noise and flickering lights and blurringly fast motion as the ship created thousands of new machines to do . . . who-knew-what.

Most of the engineering space wasn't even filled with air; the material, components and machines could move faster that way. Gravious was flying down a transparent traveltube set into the ceiling. Nine kilometres of that took it to a wall which led into the relative serenity – or at least, stillness – of the sea battle tableau. It was half way across that now; just another four thousand metres to go.

From *Excession* by Iain M Banks

Atmosphere

AF1
You should be able to experiment with **figurative language** in conveying a sense of character and setting.

You can create a particular **atmosphere** through your description of the **setting** of a story. To create atmosphere you need to think carefully about the **vocabulary**, **imagery** and **sentence structure** you use in your writing. Look at the following descriptions of a beach and decide what kind of atmosphere is being created.

Dark, brooding clouds bruised the sky. Rain battered the cliffs. The wind howled as if in pain, filling my brain with the terrible memories of my last visit to the beach.

Wispy clouds scudded across the sun as the wind whipped playfully against deckchair canvas.

The sun smiled down from a bright, cloudless sky. Children's laughter mingled with the lively shouts of excited seagulls.

Creating tension and suspense

Read the following extract and think about how character description and behaviour, use of language and structure help to create **tension**.

The narrator begins very confidently, but by the end of the extract he begins to sound doubtful.

Repeated warnings

Formal, old fashioned and complicated style of speech gives clues about the character – pompous and arrogant

Early clues that the house is haunted

Unpleasant character description

Repeated descriptive detail

'I can assure you,' said I, 'that it will take a very tangible ghost to frighten me.' And I stood up before the fire with my glass in my hand.

'It is your own choosing,' said **the man with the withered arm**, and glanced at me askance.

'Eight-and-twenty years,' said I, 'I have lived, and never a ghost have I seen as yet.'

The old woman sat staring hard into the fire, her pale eyes wide open. 'Ah,' she broke in: 'and eight-and-twenty years you have lived and never seen the likes of this house, I reckon. There's a many things to see, when one's still but eight-and-twenty.' She swayed her head slowly from side to side. 'A many thing to see and sorrow for.'

I half suspected the old people were trying to enhance the **spiritual terrors of their house** by their droning insistence. I put down my empty glass on the table and looked about the room, and caught a glimpse of myself, abbreviated and broadened to an impossible sturdiness, in the queer old mirror at the end of the room. 'Well,' I said, 'if I see anything tonight, I shall be so much the wiser. For I come to the business with an open mind.'

'It's your own choosing,' said **the man with the withered arm** once more.

I heard the sound of a stick and a shambling step on the flags in the passage outside, and the door creaked on its hinges as **a second old man entered, more bent, more wrinkled, more aged even than the first. He supported himself by a single crutch, his eyes were covered by a shade, and his lower lip, half averted, hung pale and pink from his decaying yellow teeth. He made straight for an armchair on the opposite side of the table, sat down clumsily, and began to cough.** The man with the withered arm gave this newcomer a short glance of positive dislike; the old woman took no notice of his arrival, but remained with her eyes fixed steadily on the fire.

'I said – it's your own choosing,' said **the man with the withered arm**, when the coughing had ceased for a while.

'It's my own choosing,' I answered.

The man with the shade became aware of my presence for the first time, and threw his head back for a moment and sideways, to see me. I caught a momentary glimpse of his eyes, small and bright and inflamed. Then he began to cough and splutter again.

'Why don't you drink?' said **the man with the withered arm**, pushing the beer towards him. The man with the shade poured out a glassful with a shaky arm that splashed half as much again on the deal table. **A monstrous shadow of him crouched upon the wall and mocked his action as he poured and drank. I must confess I had scarce expected these grotesque custodians.**

From *The Red Room* by H G Wells

> Description that emphasises the dim lighting and shadows.

Glossary

tangible – real
askance – to look with suspicion or disapproval
enhance the spiritual terrors – exaggerate the ghostly nature of the house
averted – hidden
custodians – caretakers

AF1 AF3
You should be able to use a range of **narrative devices** to involve the reader, e.g. *withholding information*.

One of the most successful techniques H G Wells has used in this passage is **withholding information**. The reader doesn't really know who these people are, where they are or what they are doing there. This forces the reader to predict what will happen and allows the reader to be involved in the story straightaway.

Sentence level

You should be able to: **recognise some of the differences in sentence structure, vocabulary and tone between a modern English text and a text from another historical period.** Some obvious examples from *The Red Room* are:

'Eight-and-twenty years,' said I – the tone of this speech is very formal. This is because of the word order (syntax). In modern speech we would say or write: 'Twenty-eight years,' I said.

I put down my empty glass on the table and looked about the room, and caught a glimpse of myself, abbreviated and broadened to an impossible sturdiness, in the queer old mirror at the end of the room. In modern writing there is a trend towards shorter sentences and the use of fewer commas. The above sentence could be expressed as a compound sentence followed by a complex sentence, rather than just one complicated complex sentence: 'I put down my glass and looked about the room. I caught a glimpse. . .'

Progress Check

1. Syntax is the technical term for what?
2. 'Dark, brooding clouds bruised the sky.' is a complex / compound / simple sentence.
3. The sentence in question 2 uses personification. TRUE or FALSE?

1 word order 2 Simple 3 True

6.4 Writing dialogue

Dialogue is another word for **speech** or **conversation**. Most fiction contains dialogue because it allows the main characters to communicate with each other. Dialogue is important for the following reasons:

- it helps to **bring the characters to life**
- it **reveals new information** about the character speaking or the character being spoken about
- it **adds variety** to the story.

It is important to think about **how** characters say things, as well as **what** they say.

When you use dialogue in a story, think about all the different ways there are to describe **how** somebody says something. Using a variety of verbs to describe speech gives the reader more information about what a character is like. Here are some words you could use to replace **said**:

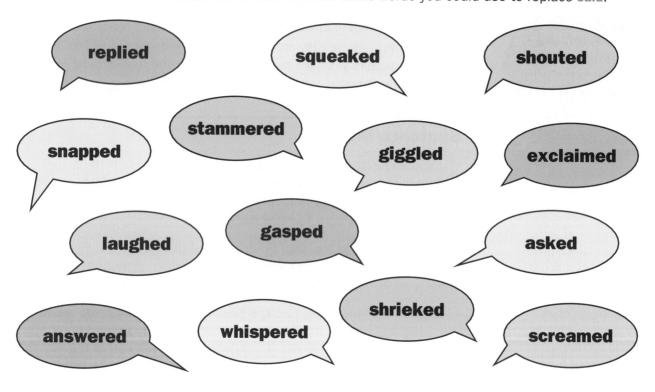

6.5 Structure

AF3
You should be able to **structure** a story with an **arresting opening**, a **developing plot**, a **complication**, a **crisis** and a **satisfying resolution**.

Your writing needs a clearly defined structure. This will usually take the form of three definite stages: **the beginning**, **the middle** and **the ending**.

The beginning

- In the opening section of a piece of imaginative writing, you need to introduce the **characters** and the **setting** and begin to **develop the main plot strands**.
- It is important to **create an interesting opening**, as you need to capture the attention of your reader.

- Do not give your reader too much detail. Keep them guessing so that they will want to read on. **Never launch straight into 'telling a story'.**
- Begin with an interesting **description of a character or the setting**.
- If you are writing a **first-person narrative**, you could begin with an intriguing statement from the narrator.

Key Point	If you can handle a more complicated structure, you could begin the story with the climax of the plot and go on to look at how the events took place. You could produce a **circular structure** by returning to the same event at the end.

The following extract, from *Kit's Wilderness* by David Almond, serves as a prologue to the main story. This opening refers to the end of the story, which gives the book a **circular structure**. It is an effective opening because it raises questions, gives the reader clues about what will happen in the story and introduces the main characters in an intriguing way.

Clue: the main characters go missing and are presumed dead.

Question: what has happened to them?

Clue: the whole community has been searching and worrying.

Intriguing introduction to and description of the main characters.

Clues: Kit is the narrator. The story is connected to the past.

Questions: What is the game? What have they been through?

Clues: the game will be important.

> **They thought we had disappeared, and they were wrong. They thought we were dead, and they were wrong.** We stumbled together out of the ancient darkness into the shining valley. The sun glared down on us. The whole world glistened with ice and snow. We held our arms against the light and stared in wonder at each other. **We were scorched and blackened from the flames. There was dried blood on our lips, cuts and bruises on our skin.** Our eyes began to burn with joy and we laughed, and touched each other and started to walk down together towards Stoneygate. Down there, our neighbours were digging for us in the snow. Policemen were dragging the river bed for us. The children saw us first and started running. Their voices echoed with astonishment and joy: 'Here they are! Oh, here they are!' They clustered around us. **They watched us as if we were ghosts, or creatures from some weird dream.** 'Here they are!' they whispered. 'Look at them. Look at the state of them!'
>
> Yes, here we were, the children who had disappeared, brought back into the world as if by magic: **John Askew, the blackened boy with bone necklaces and paintings on him; Allie Keenan, the good-bad ice girl with silver skin and claws; the wild dog Jax; and me, Kit Watson, with ancient stories in my head and ancient pebbles in my palm.**
>
> We kept on walking towards our homes with the children whispering and giggling at our side. We smiled and smiled. **Who could have known that we would walk together with such happiness, after all we'd been through? At times it seemed that there would be no end it, that there would just be darkness, that there would be no light. It started with a game, a game we played in the autumn. I played it first on the day the clocks went back.**
>
> From *Kit's Wilderness* by David Almond

Opening sentences

The opening sentences of this example are particularly effective:

They thought we had disappeared, and they were wrong. They thought we were dead, and they were wrong.

These two sentences have exactly the same structure.

Repetition of *they* and *we* suggests a battle or misunderstanding between the main characters and the community.

The sentences would make sense without the comma, but the comma emphasises the differences between 'them' and 'us'.

References to disappearance and death make the opening dramatic and powerful and raise questions immediately.

> The comma creates a caesura.

The middle

- In the central section of your writing, you need to **develop plot, characterisation and relationships**. Development is essential if you are to hold the interest of the reader.
- If you made a **character fact file** as preparation, make sure you introduce some details from it.
- **Refer back** to your character plans to make sure that they react to events in the way their personalities suggest. If you have said that a character is selfish and self-obsessed, he or she wouldn't offer to help a stranger.
- Think about how you can use **language and structure** to make your writing interesting and lively.

Plot, description and dialogue

Make sure you keep a **balance between plot development, dialogue (conversation) and description**. Too much dialogue makes your writing stilted. (Remember, you are not writing a script!)

Plot

Dialogue

Description

That day after school I went out alone, climbed the fence. There were dozens of kids playing in the gathering dark. There was a slide on a bare patch of ground. Someone had brought a lantern down. They slid through its pale glow, clashed into each other, went sprawling, laughed and squealed.

'Kit!' someone yelled. 'Come and play, Kit!'

Then screamed: 'Aaaaaaaa! Hahaha!'

I waved and walked on. The frosted grass crunched and crackled under my feet. The houselights from the opposite bank shimmered on the slow river. Stars brightened as the dark came on. No moon. I looked down and was certain I saw ice forming there at the river's edge. Cold enough, I thought. Bitter cold.

I closed my eyes, saw Grandpa as a boy, slipping and sliding on the ice. I smiled to myself, then heard a whispering, a tiny giggling nearby. Opened my eyes, saw nothing.

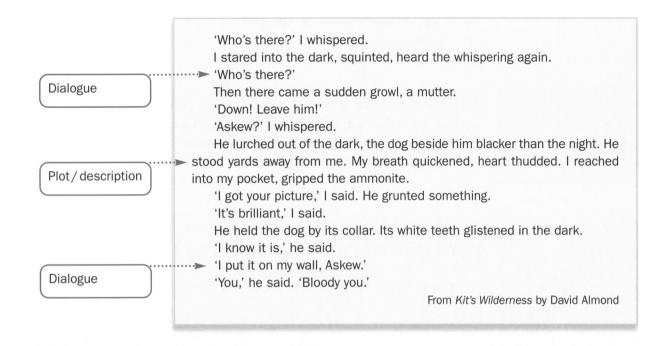

Dialogue

'Who's there?' I whispered.
I stared into the dark, squinted, heard the whispering again.
'Who's there?'
Then there came a sudden growl, a mutter.
'Down! Leave him!'
'Askew?' I whispered.

Plot / description

He lurched out of the dark, the dog beside him blacker than the night. He stood yards away from me. My breath quickened, heart thudded. I reached into my pocket, gripped the ammonite.
'I got your picture,' I said. He grunted something.
'It's brilliant,' I said.
He held the dog by its collar. Its white teeth glistened in the dark.
'I know it is,' he said.

Dialogue

'I put it on my wall, Askew.'
'You,' he said. 'Bloody you.'

From *Kit's Wilderness* by David Almond

Key Point

Notice how many different verbs are used to describe how things are said: **yelled, screamed, whispered**.
Sometimes you don't need to add he said / she said; this helps to maintain the rhythm of the conversation.

The ending

In the final section of your writing, you must begin to tie up loose ends. You have three main options for finishing your writing:

- **a cliffhanger**
- **a twist in the tale**
- **a resolution**.

Cliffhanger

With a cliffhanger, the story ends **without conclusion** or **resolution**. This keeps the reader guessing as to what will happen next. However, you need to **leave some clues** and have some ideas yourself about what will happen next. You should **plan** to finish in this way rather than realising you have run out of time. An unfinished ending and a cliffhanger ending are two completely different things!

Twist in the tale

A twist in the tale is a completely **unexpected** twist in the plot, right at the end. This is an exciting way to end a story but it is also more difficult to manage. Again, it is important to **plan** for this kind of ending.

Resolution

With a resolution, all the loose ends are tied up and the ending is **complete and definite**. This would often be a happy ending, but it doesn't have to be.

Try to avoid clichéd endings. You could really ruin a good story for want of an original conclusion. For example avoid, 'Then I woke up. It had all been a dream!'

Key Point	Time spent planning is time well spent. In an exam situation you should take between five and ten minutes to think about **what** you are going to write and **how** you are going to sustain your narrative. You should also plan how your story is going to end.

Progress Check	① Dialogue is another word for. . . ② You should develop plot, characterisation and relationships at the **beginning / middle / ending** of a story. ③ A story that ends without resolution is a **cliffhanger / twist in the tale** ending. 1 Conversation 2 Middle 3 Cliffhanger **Have a go** Plan the structure for a story about a journey to a new and unfamiliar place. ① Write the opening sentences. ② Decide on which kind of ending you will use. ③ Write five main bullet points for each section. Think about: **characters, setting, plot developments, relationship developments and language.**

6.6 Narrative perspective

AF3
You should be able to explore different ways of opening, structuring and ending narratives and experiment with narrative perspective.

It is possible to manipulate the reader by experimenting with different **narrative voices**.

Third-person narrative

In **third-person narrative**, the narrator is someone who is outside the story and refers to all the characters by name or he / she. This style of narration allows you to show more than one perspective.

An **omniscient narrator** is a narrator who knows everything about the situations and characters (and their feelings) in a story. This allows the narrator to let the reader into the inner thoughts and feelings of the characters and to comment on them. It also means that the narrator can give information about what will happen later in the story so that the **reader knows more than the characters**.

First-person narrative

First-person narrative usually looks at situations from only one point of view. This means that the narrator can **manipulate** the reader's sympathies by emphasising particular aspects of a story or leaving out information. A first-person narrator can be somebody who relates a story as they have observed it, a minor participant in the story they are relating, or a central character in the story. Kit Watson is the narrator and central character in *Kit's Wilderness*.

Dual narrative

The following extract is from a novel called *Stone Cold* by Robert Swindells. In this novel there is a **dual narrative**: the same story is told by Link, a homeless teenager and Shelter, a psychopathic killer who targets homeless people. Placing the **two stories side by side** shows two contrasting points of view on the same subject. As the story progresses, the characters and their stories sometimes meet and start to weave together and then diverge again. This is effective because it shows the danger that the unsuspecting Link is in.

According to Link and his friend Ginger, **solcredulists** are people who believe everything they read in *The Sun* newspaper.

For something to do, I began studying their various responses. Some would simply walk on glassy-eyed and expressionless, as though Ginger wasn't there. Some assumed angry expressions, compressing their lips and sweeping by as though grossly insulted. There were head-shakers, pocket-patters and shruggers, who demonstrated through mime the absence of coins in their pockets; and there were those who'd mutter unintelligibly, so that you couldn't tell whether they'd said sorry no change or bugger off. Once Ginger accosted a stiff, military-looking guy who stopped, looked him up and down as if he was something the cat sicked up and said, 'Change? I'd change you my lad, if I had you in khaki for six weeks.' There were a lot of **solcredulists** about.

Daily Routine Orders 8

It has happened again. I was on my way to inspect theatreland when two dossers approached me. One – the scruffier of the two – asked me for change. I responded in my usual way, and as I passed on I distinctly heard them laughing. I hope for their sakes that they manage to retain that sense of humour because they'll need it quite soon. I never forget a face, and our next meeting will prove far more amusing for me than for them.

By golly it will.

From *Stone Cold* by Robert Swindells

Word level

Omniscient means knowing everything.

The prefix **omni-** means **all**, from the Latin *omnis* meaning **all**: **omni**potent – all powerful, **omni**vorous – feeds on many kinds of food.

Use a dictionary to check that the following words have something to do with all or everything: omnibus, omnidirectional, omnipresent.

Progress Check

1　In third-person narrative, the narrator takes part in the story. TRUE or FALSE?
2　A dual narrative tells the same story from more than one point of view. TRUE or FALSE?
3　Omniscient means: a) all powerful b) all knowing c) everywhere

1 False　2 True　3 b) All knowing

Have a go

Try writing the same story from different narrative perspectives. How does it change the story?

Assessment questions

The following question will help you to prepare for the **Optional Tests** and **APP tasks**.

1. 'Lots of people believe in ghosts and the supernatural.'

   Write three or four paragraphs of a story including: dialogue, action, description of characters and setting to create a tense or frightening atmosphere.

2. 'It wasn't me!'

   Write about someone wrongly suspected or accused of committing a crime.

   Think about:
   ● what they have been accused of
   ● how that person would feel
   ● what happens to them.

3. Write about a frightening encounter with an animal.

   ● Try to build up a feeling of tension or suspense.
   ● Describe the animal.

4. Write about being lost or followed in a forest.

   ● Try to build up an atmosphere of fear.
   ● Describe the forest.
   ● Write in the first or third person.

The Writing Papers of the Optional Tests will assess your responses across all of the Assessment Focuses for Writing (listed on page 157). Your teacher may use APP to assess one or more of the Assessment Focuses in your ongoing work or in specific tasks. If you have been set a specific task, your teacher will usually tell you which Assessment Focuses will be targeted.

When you attempt the questions on this page you should decide whether to concentrate on an Assessment Focus you know you need to improve on or whether to test your skills across all of the AFs.

7 Writing to inform, instruct, explain and describe

After studying this section you should be able to:

- write to inform
- write to instruct
- write to explain
- write to describe

To achieve the following National Curriculum levels you need to do the following for each level.

Level 4
- **Sustain** and **develop** your ideas.
- **Organise** your ideas appropriately **to suit a range of purposes**.

Level 5
- Make your **meaning clear** in a range of forms.
- Use a more **formal style** where appropriate.
- Make **adventurous vocabulary** choices.
- Organise your writing into paragraphs and make clear links between them.

Level 6
- Use an **impersonal style** where appropriate.
- Use a **range of sentence structures** to create effects.
- Control and sequence your writing.

Level 7
- Consistently **match your writing style to the purpose** and **audience** of your writing.
- Use **paragraphing** and **punctuation** to make the **sequence of ideas coherent** to the reader.

7.1 Writing to inform

Conventions of information texts

Information texts are written in the **present tense** and the **third person**. Sentences are usually **simple** and **compound** to present information in a straightforward way. Information texts use the following devices: **sub-headings, pictures, charts** and **tables**.

The text on page 97 conforms to most of the conventions of an information text.

Key Point

Common information texts are: leaflets, textbooks and encyclopaedia entries.

Environment

Food Chains

A **food chain** describes the feeding relationship between living organisms in a habitat. It also shows how energy and **biomass** are transferred along the food chain when the organisms feed.

Biomass refers to the total mass (quantity) of organic material at each stage in the chain, not the number of organisms.

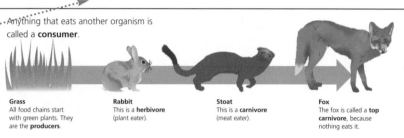

Anything that eats another organism is called a **consumer**.

Grass
All food chains start with green plants. They are the **producers**.

Rabbit
This is a **herbivore** (plant eater).

Stoat
This is a **carnivore** (meat eater).

Fox
The fox is called a **top carnivore**, because nothing eats it.

Pyramids of Biomass

Energy enters a food chain from the Sun. Some energy and biomass is lost at each stage of a food chain as faeces (solid waste), movement energy, heat energy (especially by birds and mammals).

Therefore, only a small amount of energy and biomass is incorporated into a consumer's body and transferred to the next feeding level. This is shown in

a **pyramid of biomass**.

In the pyramid of biomass below, the loss of energy and biomass at each stage is indicated, and illustrates why such a representation of a food chain is always pyramid-shaped. This pyramid of biomass describes the food chain above quantitatively (amount of biomass), so it is more accurate than a food chain.

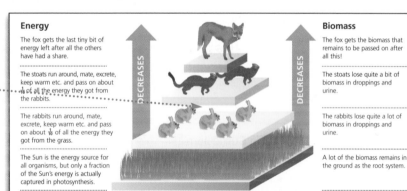

Energy

The fox gets the last tiny bit of energy left after all the others have had a share.

The stoats run around, mate, excrete, keep warm etc. and pass on about $\frac{1}{10}$ of all the energy they got from the rabbits.

The rabbits run around, mate, excrete, keep warm etc. and pass on about $\frac{1}{10}$ of all the energy they got from the grass.

The Sun is the energy source for all organisms, but only a fraction of the Sun's energy is actually captured in photosynthesis.

DECREASES

DECREASES

Biomass

The fox gets the biomass that remains to be passed on after all this!

The stoats lose quite a bit of biomass in droppings and urine.

The rabbits lose quite a lot of biomass in droppings and urine.

A lot of the biomass remains in the ground as the root system.

④

Side annotations:

Written in present tense

Uses third person

Uses sub-headings

Length of sentences is decided by the need for clarity – mostly simple and compound sentences

Examples, diagrams and illustrations back up the information in the text

---

Writing your own information text

AF3
You should be able to organise and present information, selecting and synthesising appropriate material and guiding the reader clearly through the text.

There are three main steps to follow when writing your own information text. Follow these steps to write an information text about your school.

Planning

The first thing you need to do is to decide on the categories of information you are going to provide, for example by making a spider diagram like the one on the next page.

Key Point   Remember to write in the third person and the present tense.

Writing

Your writing style needs to be clear, factual and formal. As you are required to write in the third person, you should use terms such as: '**students study** a wide range of subjects'. **Don't** use **we** or **I**: 'at school **we study** lots of different subjects'.

Look at this short example of writing about the lessons that take place in a particular school. Instead of giving this the title 'Lessons', you could use a more **formal** expression like 'The Curriculum'

> The Curriculum
> In Year 7, students follow a full programme of National Curriculum subjects, including Religious Education, Drama and ICT. In Years 8 and 9 students are given the opportunity to enhance their language skills by following courses in both French and German.

Visual variety

Remember that a successful information text needs to hold the reader's attention. Think about ways you can improve the visual impact of your information text:

- **bullet points**
- **pictures**
- **headings**
- different **font sizes and styles**
- **colour**
- **tables, charts** and **graphs**.

So, for example, when you are writing about your school you might present recent exam results in a graph or chart, and uniform details as a bullet pointed list, e.g.

GCSE examination results

% A*–C grades achieved

Art 82%
English 55%
Mathematics 53%

Lower School Girls Uniform:
- Navy skirt
- White shirt
- Navy and gold school tie (ties may be bought from the school office)
- Plain navy v-neck jumper
- Navy blazer with school badge
- Navy tights or white socks

When does information become persuasion?

Remember that many texts have **more than one purpose**. This means that **information** can sometimes be presented in a **persuasive way**. Read the example below; it is an information leaflet about a holiday home that is available to rent. As well as giving information about the house and its location, it clearly aims to persuade the people who read it to rent the house for their next holiday.

'Waterside', Poole, Dorset

A 5-bedroom detached property set in a stunning beachside location. Fully equipped with all amenities and set over 3 levels, the property boasts a huge kitchen, dining room, integrated garage, two living rooms which both boast large-screen LCD televisions, DVD, CD, and satellite TV.

On the second floor are 3 double bedrooms, each with en-suite, balcony and fitted wardrobes, while the third floor has 2 single bedrooms, office, child's toy room and a further bathroom.

PRICES (based on a one-week stay)

03.01–27.03	28.03–03.07	04.07–25.09	26.09–29.12
£555	£635	£785	£575

BEDS	SLEEPS	EN-SUITE	PARKING	TV/DVD	SMOKING
5	8	YES	YES	YES	NO

Thinkstock

7.2 Writing to instruct

Instruction texts include: **directions, rules for playing games, recipes, manuals** (DIY, etc.).

Giving clear instructions

Read the following description of how to make beans on toast. Is it a useful set of instructions for making beans on toast? If not, why not?

How to make beans on toast

I don't know much about cooking, but I can make beans on toast. The toast should be golden brown and really hot. You can cook the toast in a toaster or under the grill. I always burn my fingers on the grill, so I like to use the toaster – I love the noise it makes when it pops up! You can use butter or margarine on your toast, but I like butter best, especially if there are little air holes in the bread so the melted butter drips on your fingers – yum! I should have mentioned that while you are cooking your toast you need to cook the beans, otherwise your toast will be cold and soggy – yuck!! So put the beans in a saucepan and turn the heat up quite high. Of course, you need to take the beans out of the tin before you cook them. Make sure that you don't have too much heat because you should try not to boil or burn the beans. When they are hot enough – don't stick your finger in to test them because you could burn it – put the beans on the toast and enjoy!

There are many problems with this recipe. The main problems are:

- it is **disorganised**
- it is **difficult to follow** because it's all one paragraph and doesn't have clear steps
- it contains **personal opinion**
- it is too **conversational**.

This 'recipe' can't really be described as an instructional text as it breaks nearly all the rules listed below.

Conventions of instruction texts

Instruction texts:

- are written in the **imperative**
- are written in the **present tense**
- can include some sentences containing '**you**' but shouldn't use '**I**'
- have **short sentences**, each covering one instruction
- use **connectives** related to time or chronology, e.g. **then**, **next**
- punctuation is limited to **commas** and **full stops**
- don't contain personal information or anecdote (stories)
- don't use emotive language to describe the product
- are presented in **logical steps**, in **short paragraphs** that can be numbered
- often **begin with a list** of ingredients, materials, equipment
- include a **title or statement** of what is to be achieved.

Now read the following recipe. The way it is written makes it clearer and more effective.

> **AF2**
>
> You should be able to write instructions which are helpfully sequenced and signposted and deploy a range of imperative verbs.

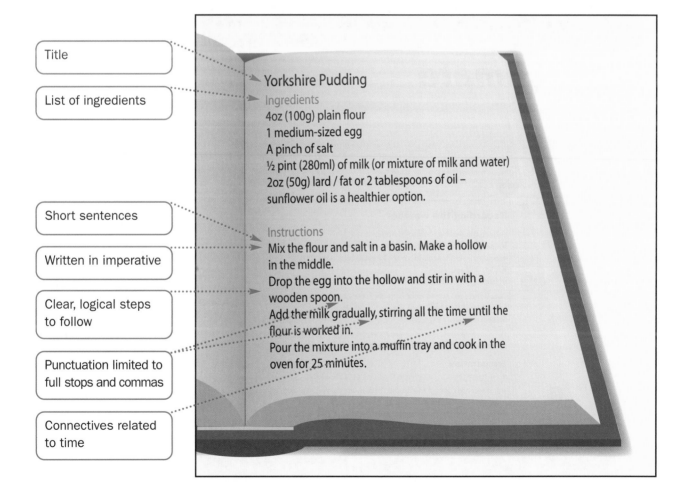

Title

List of ingredients

Short sentences

Written in imperative

Clear, logical steps to follow

Punctuation limited to full stops and commas

Connectives related to time

Yorkshire Pudding

Ingredients
4oz (100g) plain flour
1 medium-sized egg
A pinch of salt
½ pint (280ml) of milk (or mixture of milk and water)
2oz (50g) lard / fat or 2 tablespoons of oil –
sunflower oil is a healthier option.

Instructions
Mix the flour and salt in a basin. Make a hollow in the middle.
Drop the egg into the hollow and stir in with a wooden spoon.
Add the milk gradually, stirring all the time until the flour is worked in.
Pour the mixture into a muffin tray and cook in the oven for 25 minutes.

1. Which punctuation mark should have been avoided in the beans on toast recipe?
2. When making beans on toast, you need to make the toast and cook the beans at the same time. Which of the following connectives would be most useful to explain this: **first**, **meanwhile**, **finally**?
3. Identify **two** imperative verbs in the recipe for Yorkshire Pudding.

1 Exclamation mark 2 Meanwhile 3 Mix, make, drop, stir, add, pour, cook

Have a go
Write your own recipe for making beans on toast.

7.3 Writing to explain

Conventions of an explanation text

The text below conforms to most of the conventions of an **explanation text**.

Chapter 5

Weather and climate

Weather

1 **KEY POINT** Weather describes the atmospheric conditions at a particular place and time together with the changes taking place over the short term (hour-by-hour or day-by-day).

Recording the weather

Data on the weather is obtained from:
- daily readings of instruments at a weather station
- automatic instruments in remote locations (e.g. ocean buoys)
- ships and aeroplanes
- satellites and radar images.

Data is recorded at least once every 24 hours. The information is plotted on maps or synoptic charts, then analysed to obtain a weather forecast.
Meteorologists are responsible for recording and analysing the weather.

A range of data is recorded

Temperature
- Air temperature is recorded in the shade (in a Stevenson's Screen).
- It is recorded using a **maximum/minimum thermometer** (highest and lowest temperatures in the last 24 hours).
- It is recorded in degrees **centigrade** (Celsius) or **Fahrenheit**.

1 The opening contains a **general statement** to introduce the topic.
2 The text uses the **passive voice**.
3 Uses **connectives** that indicate **sequence**.
4 The text is written in the **present tense**.

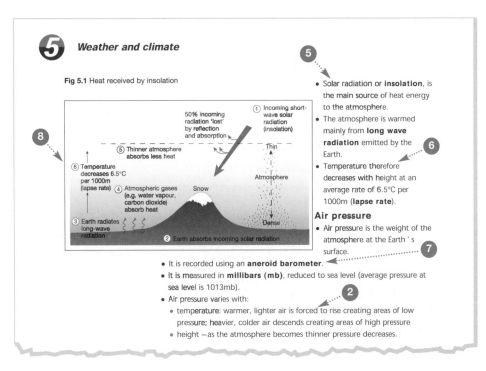

⑤ Weather and climate

Fig 5.1 Heat received by insolation

⑤
- Solar radiation or **insolation**, is the main source of heat energy to the atmosphere.
- The atmosphere is warmed mainly from **long wave radiation** emitted by the Earth.
- Temperature therefore decreases with height at an average rate of 6.5°C per 1000m (**lapse rate**).

Air pressure
- Air pressure is the weight of the atmosphere at the Earth's surface.
- It is recorded using an **aneroid barometer**.
- It is measured in **millibars (mb)**, reduced to sea level (average pressure at sea level is 1013mb).
- Air pressure varies with:
  - temperature: warmer, lighter air is forced to rise creating areas of low pressure; heavier, colder air descends creating areas of high pressure
  - height — as the atmosphere becomes thinner pressure decreases.

⑤ The development of the explanation draws attention to **how** something works or **why** something happens.

⑥ Uses **connectives** that indicate **cause and effect**.

⑦ **Technical vocabulary** gives the piece quite a formal style.

⑧ Uses **diagrams** to explain processes.

Connectives word bank

AF5
You should be able to use a range of link words and phrases to signpost texts, including links of time (*then*, *later*, *meanwhile*) and cause (*so*, *because*, *since*).

Use the following **connectives** in your own writing.

Cause and effect	Sequence	Comparison
because	then	similarly
so	next	whereas
due to	gradually	on the other hand
as a result of	finally	by contrast
therefore		however

Sentence level

- **Active voice** – in an active sentence, the subject or agent performs the verb, which is received by the object: **agent – verb – recipient**.

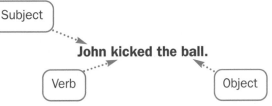

- **Passive voice** – in a passive sentence, the sentence is turned around so that the normal object of a sentence becomes the subject: **recipient – verb – agent**.

> ### Sentence level continued
>
> The **active voice** is more common than the **passive voice**, which can sometimes seem clumsy or unnatural.
>
> However, the passive voice can omit the agent, and this kind of sentence can be quite useful. Leaving out the agent allows the writer to conceal who is responsible for an action, e.g. **The ball was kicked. The window was smashed**.

Progress Check

Complete the explanation sentences in 1–3 by adding a connective and a reason.

1. Jane decided not to go out last night . . . .
2. The number of people using public transport has fallen . . .
3. Simon achieved less than 50% in the test . . .
4. What is different about this explanation sentence? *As a result of prolonged rainfall, the river burst its banks.*

(Answers to 1–3 are only possibilities.) 1 Because she had too much work to do 2 Due to rising fares 3 So he had to re-sit it 4 The connective is at the beginning of the sentence.

7.4 Writing to describe

Describing people

When you describe a person, you might choose to emphasise a particular feature of his or her **appearance** or **personality**. For example: 'My primary school teacher, Mrs Bell, wore brown shoes. She was very kind and rarely shouted.'

To make a piece of writing more interesting, think about other words and phrases you could add to the description to give more information. Try to vary your sentence structure too.

First sentence simple

These words describe the person as well as the shoes

My primary school teacher, Mrs Bell, wore **sensible, sturdy, brown** lace up shoes. She was very kind and **always had a smile for everyone**. She rarely shouted and, because of this, **you** knew you were really in trouble if she did.

Second sentence compound

Use of second person to involve the reader

Suggests generosity and fairness

Third sentence complex

If you are asked to describe a person in detail, you need to think about lots of **different aspects** of that person, not just what they look like.

A person I remember clearly from my childhood is my next-door neighbour, Elsie. She was the oldest person I knew. Her skin was like crinkly brown paper and her eyes watered when she laughed. She had delicate, mottled hands and her wedding ring was loose on her finger.

She was generous and kind. Whenever we visited we had jelly sweets or Jaffa cakes. She called me 'wench' or 'ducks'. She always seemed to be washing sheets and took great pride in always being the first out to hang washing on the line.

Describing places

The following is a fictional description. The techniques used in narrative writing can also be used in descriptive non-fiction.

Look out for:
- **imagery** – personification, simile, etc.
- **original and adventurous vocabulary**
- **amusing detail**
- **varied sentence structure**
- **sensory description**.

> Interesting and adventurous vocabulary choice

> Interesting vocabulary choice – gives an immediate impression of the house

> The house is personified – it shuts out the light and refuses to let it in

The house in which they lived was a large, old house. Esme had heard people describe it as **ramshackle** and **dilapidated**. It was a big, dark house that seemed more than just a little out of place among the trails of modern housing developments that surrounded it. Its blackened walls and narrow windows ensured that **it shut out** the light, and even on a mid-summer's day, when the sun shone brightly, the house **refused to let it in**. The **crumbling**

Detail to emphasise the state of the house

Range of verbs to describe objects' movement

Simple sentence

Complex sentence

chimney leaned precariously to the left, the narrow windows were filthy, the grass well overgrown and the paint on the old wooden front door was dull and chipped, exposing ugly patches of pond-green paint underneath. A dead plant **slumped** in a pot by the front door, **as though it had given up the will to live** long ago, whilst at the bottom of the stone steps, torn pages from an old newspaper **flapped** in the wind.

Esme thought that it was a most unusual house. It was a house that held secrets. And despite its distinct lack of charm, there was something oddly appealing about it.

Amusing description

Key Point	A good description should bring a person to life or allow the readers to visualise themselves in the place or situation described.

Describing memories

AF1
You should be able to describe an object, person or setting in a way that includes relevant details and is accurate and evocative.

When you write about a memory, you may have to describe people, places and objects. The plan below is a **brainstorm** for writing about a journey.

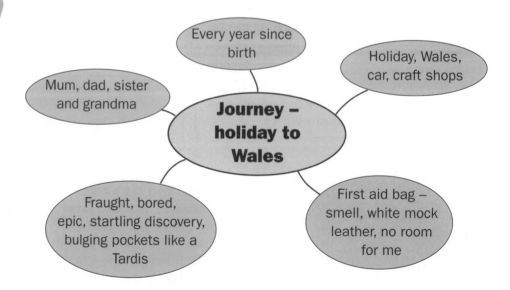

Every year since birth

Holiday, Wales, car, craft shops

Mum, dad, sister and grandma

Journey – holiday to Wales

Fraught, bored, epic, startling discovery, bulging pockets like a Tardis

First aid bag – smell, white mock leather, no room for me

Now look at how this planning has been used to start a piece of writing.

Dramatic choice of vocabulary to draw the reader in

Rhetorical question, involves the reader

Shorter sentence contrasts with the longer descriptive sentences

Vocabulary choice

Inclusion of humour

Simile

Adjective choices

At the age of fourteen I made a **startling discovery** – I only lived two hours away from the North Wales seaside town that had been the scene of many a happy family holiday. **The reason for my surprise?** From birth I had taken that same **epic journey** every year and our previous record was seven hours! My grandma always came on holiday with us and she is not the best traveller. As a result of this, I am familiar with every public toilet and small tearoom on our route. Delightful as they are, if you miss them out of the grand tour it takes hours off the journey time!

Our preparation for the journey always reminded me of the old joke: 'how many elephants can you fit into a mini?' Answer: none if you're going on holiday with us! Every available inch of space, including the **Tardis-like side pockets**, was filled with bodies and essential beach holiday equipment.

As I was the youngest and smallest, I had to sit in the middle, sandwiched between my **fraught** mother and **bored** sister. I had to fold myself up, knees jammed under my chin. There wasn't any floor space because the first aid kit took up all the room. The first aid kit was **a white, mock leather, draw string bag that smelt of mothballs and camphor**. The smell of the bag always made feel a bit sick, which was unfortunate considering its purpose.

Object detail – extended noun phrase to make the sentence more interesting
Sensory memory

Progress Check

1 When you are describing a person, you should concentrate on what they look like. TRUE or FALSE?
2 The techniques used in fiction and non-fiction description are completely different. TRUE or FALSE?
3 Imagery such as s_____ and m_____ can be used in descriptive writing.

1 False 2 False 3 Similes and metaphors

Have a go
Write a description of your bedroom, experimenting with some of the techniques discussed above.

Assessment questions

The following questions will help you to prepare for the **Optional Tests** and **APP tasks**.

1. Write a set of **instructions** to get from your house to your school.

2. Write an **information text** about teenage fashions. Write **three** or **four** paragraphs.

3. **Describe** your ideal holiday location. Write **three** or **four** paragraphs.

4. **Describe** a place you have enjoyed visiting.
    You could write about:
    - when and why you visited the place
    - why you liked it
    - what the place is like
    - why you would recommend other people to go there.

5. Many teenagers have to face important or difficult decisions. **Explain** your reasons for making a difficult decision.
    You could write about:
    - what the decision was
    - your options
    - your reasons for making the decision
    - the effects of your decision.

6. Write an **information** leaflet for teenagers on the dangers of smoking or drinking.
    You could write about:
    - the physical effects
    - reasons why young people drink or smoke
    - how to stop or control smoking or drinking.

The Writing Papers of the Optional Tests will assess your responses across all of the Assessment Focuses for Writing (listed on page 157). Your teacher may use APP to assess one or more of the Assessment Focuses in your ongoing work or in specific tasks. If you have been set a specific task, your teacher will usually tell you which Assesment Focuses will be targeted.

When you attempt the questions on this page you should decide whether to concentrate on an Assessment Focus you know you need to improve on or whether to test your skills across all of the AFs.

8 Writing to persuade and argue

After studying this section you should be able to:

- write persuasive letters
- write persuasive speeches
- present persuasive arguments
- present discursive arguments

To achieve the following National Curriculum levels you need to do the following for each level.

Level 4
- **Organise** your **ideas** clearly.
- **Interest** and **convince** your reader.

Level 5
- Use a **formal style** where appropriate.
- Use a **range of evidence** to support your ideas.
- Choose **vocabulary** to **create particular effects**.

Level 6
- **Develop** and **sustain** your argument.
- Use **sentence structure** and **punctuation** to clarify meaning and create effects.

Level 7
- Write in a **clear** and **fluent** style to persuade or advise, showing an appreciation of **audience** and **purpose**.
- **Anticipate** and **respond to** a range of counter-arguments.

There are many forms of persuasive writing; some are more obviously persuasive than others. In **Chapter 4 Reading non-fiction** you will find examples of **media** persuasive texts: **leaflets (4.3)** and **advertisements (4.4)**. These texts are often designed to persuade the reader to buy something, and therefore the persuasive devices are quite easily identified.

In this chapter a more **formal** style of **persuasion** is explored. **Letters, speeches** and **formal arguments** are often written to persuade the reader to change their opinion about something. You will learn how to employ persuasive devices in your own writing and to manipulate your sentence structure to make your message or argument more powerful.

Key Point	Most persuasive texts use some or all of the following devices: **emotive language, repetition, rhetorical questions, presenting opinion as fact.**

8.1 Persuasive letters

Letters are often intended to be persuasive. Some examples of **persuasive letters** are:

- charity or **campaign letters**
- **letters to newspapers** expressing an opinion
- a **letter of application** for a job.

Writing a formal letter

There are lots of **conventions** to follow when writing a formal letter.

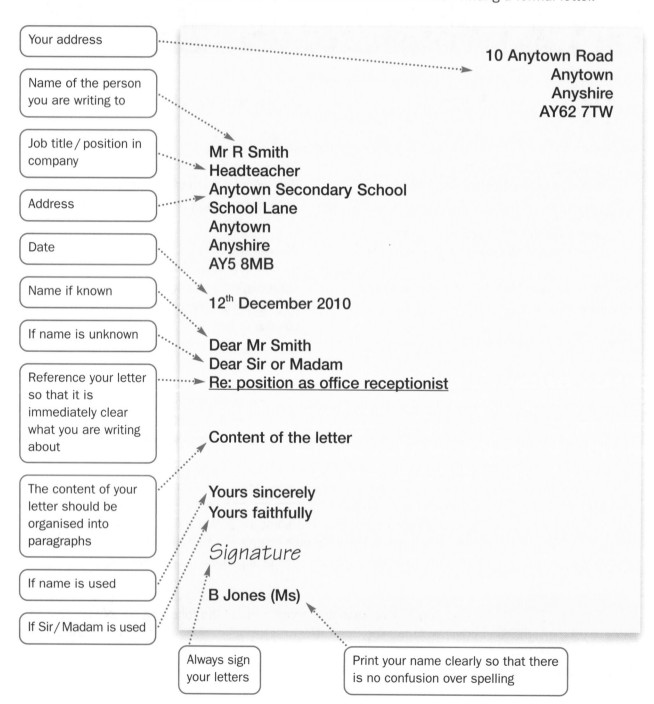

Your address	10 Anytown Road Anytown Anyshire AY62 7TW
Name of the person you are writing to	Mr R Smith
Job title / position in company	Headteacher
Address	Anytown Secondary School School Lane Anytown Anyshire AY5 8MB
Date	12th December 2010
Name if known	Dear Mr Smith
If name is unknown	Dear Sir or Madam
Reference your letter so that it is immediately clear what you are writing about	Re: position as office receptionist
	Content of the letter
The content of your letter should be organised into paragraphs	Yours sincerely
If name is used	Yours faithfully
If Sir / Madam is used	Signature
	B Jones (Ms)

Always sign your letters

Print your name clearly so that there is no confusion over spelling

Mrs Jones
12 The High Street
Holme
HD9 9ZZ

AEIOU/1234567

**Friends of
the Earth**

Fuelled by your tax, the UK's intensive meat and dairy industry is destroying the rainforest.

If that makes you angry, please act and give today.

Dear Mrs Jones

For the last few decades, UK farmers have been faced with a stark choice: to get on a brutal production line or go bust.

Factory farming means more pesticides being sprayed on farmland and more dangerous chemicals in our food. It also means UK cows, chickens and pigs being pumped full of cheap, protein-rich animal feed grown on soy plantations in South America – plantations where lush rainforest once stood.

Every tree destroyed to grow soy means more climate-changing gases are released into the atmosphere, accelerating global warming. And in another sickening twist, these plantations force indigenous people off their land and into desperate poverty.

And what is most galling of all, our taxes keep the whole system going!

If that makes you livid, we need you to demand action from your MP and make a donation to our Food Chain Campaign. Let me explain why in more detail.

The deadly food chain

Last year, our Food Chain Campaign was launched to combat the destructive process I've just described. So far, we've made enormous progress, with more than 250 MPs supporting our vision for farming – that's nearly 40 per cent of the House of Commons – but we've got to keep up the political pressure.

Here are some killer stats that reveal the true scale of the problem:
• If left to grow unchecked, soy farming and cattle ranching will destroy 40 per cent of the Amazon rainforest by 2005.
• £700 million of our tax is spent to keep it all going each year.

Clearly the system has to change.

To save the planet, we need nothing short of a revolution in agriculture, business and the economy. And that's where Friends of the Earth come in.

Respond today and force the political parties to act

I know that sometimes it's possible to get disheartened. Rarely have people felt so disenfranchised by the political process: believing that the main political parties are all talk when it comes to the environment and offer no radical alternative to the status quo. If you have little enthusiasm for the coming election, you're certainly not the only one!

It's our campaign that represents the real and lasting change the environment needs – no matter what party ends up in power.

Your support is absolutely crucial. Without you we won't be able to fund the credible and authoritative research we need to make a strong case for our practical solutions. We won't be able to publish new research showing how soy is driving deforestation in South America or produce a workable vision for planet-friendly farming in the UK.

With your help, we can reach out to more farmers and get them to speak out. And with their backing, we can persuade the Government to show leadership and fix the whole food chain in the UK and overseas. It's time to think and act globally.

Thank you again for all of your support.

Yours sincerely

Sandra Bell

Sandra Bell
Food and Farming Campaigner

Whatever you give today will make a difference. It will enable us to fund research into planet-friendly farming, help poor communities protest peacefully against big companies, and convince politicians to fix the food chain.

Please respond now.

iStockphoto / Thinkstock

Friends of the Earth England, Wales and Northern Ireland, 26-28 Underwood Street, London N1 7JQ Telephone 020 7490 1555 Fax 020 7490 0881
Website www.foe.co.uk Friends of the Earth Trust Company number 1533942 Registered Charity number 281681 Friends of the Earth Limited Company number 1012357

Persuasive devices used in the letter

- There are many examples of **emotive language** in this letter. Words and phrases have been chosen to make the UK's meat and dairy industry seem to be potentially harmful, as well as bad for the environment: *brutal production line; sickening twist; more dangerous chemicals in our food...*
- The writer of this letter has used **facts** persuasively: £700 million of our tax is spent to keep it all going each year. The use of *our tax* and *each year* highlight that it is **our** money being spent and that it is continuous – year after year.
- The use of colour and the image in the letter highlight the topic, whilst the larger white text on a green background sums up what the letter is about and how the readers' donations could make a difference.
- **Personal pronouns** are used effectively to make the reader feel that they have the power to make a difference. Towards the end of the letter, it is more persuasive because it is implied that the campaign will fail without the readers' support: *Your support is absolutely crucial. Without you...* The writer uses *I*, *we* and *our* as well as *you*, which makes the letter sound more personal and highlights that both Friends of the Earth and the readers need to work together as a team.
- The final two paragraphs are effective because they suggest that the readers' help and support is vital to progress. In the penultimate paragraph there is a statement of how the campaign will fail without the readers' support. It lists what they won't be able to do: *Without you we won't be able to fund the credible and authoritive research, We won't be able to publish...* The final paragraph suggests the readers' support will lead to global change. It lists what they will be able to do: *With your help, we can reach out to more farmers, we can persuade the Government, fix the food chain in the UK and overseas.*

AF2
You should be able to **find** and **use** different ways to **validate an argument**, e.g. *statistical evidence, exemplification, testimony.*

Word level

Using the endings **-ous**, **-ious** and **-eous**.

- **-ous** is the most common ending used to form adjectives: danger → danger**ous**.
- Use **-ious** if you can hear **shus** at the end of the word, following the letters **t**, **c** or **x**: ambi**tious**, vi**cious**, an**xious**, or if you can hear **i** as a syllable: obv**ious**.
- Use **-eous** if the root ends in **-ge**: coura**ge** → coura**geous**, or if you can hear **e** as a syllable: hid**eous**.

Key Point   A **rhetorical question** doesn't require an answer.

Using rhetorical questions as a persuasive device

A **rhetorical question** does not require or expect an answer. It is used to achieve a stronger emphasis than a direct statement. The speaker or writer assumes that the answer to the question is obvious.

The question, 'How old are you?' clearly requires an answer, whereas the question, 'It makes you think, doesn't it?' assumes that the answer must be yes and doesn't require a response.

This question could be used effectively in a persuasive letter if it followed information intended to make the reader feel uncomfortable. For example:

> Many of these homeless people are children as young as 12; children who are forced to live on the streets because of abusive or neglectful family relationships. While we enjoy the comforts of home on a cold winter's night, they are enduring the cold, scrounging for food or change, feeling hungry, cold, dirty and useless. **Makes you think, doesn't it?**

Read the following extract from another charity campaign letter and think about the use of **rhetorical questions**.

> Protecting our environment is one of the most important issues that face us. **If we don't start to look after our planet now, who will? And if we don't do it now, will it be too late?**
>
> Every individual on Earth needs to accept responsibility for protecting our precious planet – its wonderful oceans and vast deserts; its polar ice caps and array of greenery; its fabulous variety of animal, insect and bird species… the list goes on.
>
> Think about the wonder of the world around you. **Do you really want to see this spoiled? Do you really want to see any part of it gone, no matter how tiny?** Gone. Extinct forever.
>
> We at EnviroProtect believe we must act now. **Otherwise, what will be left for our children? How different will their world be?**

Progress Check

1. If you begin a letter Dear Sir, you should end with Yours sincerely. TRUE or FALSE?
2. A rhetorical question does not require an answer. TRUE or FALSE?
3. Which of the following questions is mostly likely to be used rhetorically? a) What is your name? b) Why should we pay for the mistakes of others?

1 False (Yours faithfully should be used.)   2 True   3 b)

Have a go

Write two paragraphs of a persuasive letter about animal cruelty. Try to include emotive language, personal pronouns and at least one rhetorical question.

8.2 Persuasive speeches

Speeches are very important in our society and can be a very powerful way of **persuading** our listeners to change their views. As you read in **Chapter 1**, the way you deliver a speech is very important. However, in order to deliver a powerful and persuasive speech you have to write it that way first.

The speech printed on page 114 is an extract from a powerful and influential speech made in the 19th century by William Wilberforce, a British politician and leader of the movement to abolish the slave trade.

As you read the speech, look at the words and phrases highlighted in different colours and think about why they might be important.

William Wilberforce's Abolition Speech

When I consider the magnitude of the subject which I am to bring before the House – a subject, in which the interests, not of this country, nor of Europe alone, but of the whole world, and of posterity, are involved: and when I think, at the same time, on the weakness of the advocate who has undertaken this great cause – when these reflections press upon my mind, it is impossible for me not to feel both terrified and concerned at my own inadequacy to such a task. But when I reflect, however, on the encouragement which I have had, through the whole course of a long and laborious examination of this question, and how much candour I have experienced, and how conviction has increased within my own mind, in proportion as I have advanced in my labours; – when I reflect, especially, that however averse any gentleman may now be, yet we shall all be of one opinion in the end; – when I turn myself to these thoughts, I take courage – I determine to forget all my other fears, and I march forward with a firmer step in the full assurance that my cause will bear me out, and that I shall be able to justify upon the clearest principles, every resolution in my hand, the avowed end of which is, the total abolition of the slave trade. I wish exceedingly, in the outset, to guard both myself and the House from entering into the subject with any sort of passion. It is not their passions I shall appeal to – I ask only for their cool and impartial reason; and I wish not to take them by surprise, but to deliberate, point by point, upon every part of this question. I mean not to accuse any one, but to take the shame upon myself, in common, indeed, with the whole parliament of Great Britain, for having suffered this horrid trade to be carried on under their authority. We are all guilty – we ought all to plead guilty, and not to exculpate ourselves by throwing the blame on others; and I therefore deprecate every kind of reflection against the various descriptions of people who are more immediately involved in this wretched business.

Having now disposed of the first part of this subject, I must speak of the transit of the slaves in the West Indies. This I confess, in my own opinion, is the most wretched part of the whole subject. So much misery condensed in so little room, is more than the human imagination had ever before conceived. I will not accuse the Liverpool merchants: I will allow them, nay, I will believe them to be men of humanity; and I will therefore believe, if it were not for the enormous magnitude and extent of the evil which distracts their attention from individual cases, and makes them think generally, and therefore less feelingly on the subject, they would never have persisted in the trade. I verily believe therefore, if the wretchedness of any one of the many hundred Negroes stowed in each ship could be brought before their view, and remain within the sight of the African Merchant, that there is no one among them whose heart would bear it. Let any one imagine to himself 6 or 700 of these wretches chained two and two, surrounded with every object that is nauseous and disgusting, diseased, and struggling under every kind of wretchedness! How can we bear to think of such a scene as this? One would think it had been determined to heap upon them all the varieties of bodily pain, for the purpose of blunting the feelings of the mind; and yet, in this very point (to show the power of human prejudice) the situation of the slaves has been described by Mr. Norris, one of the Liverpool delegates, in a manner which, I am sure will convince the House how interest can draw a film across the eyes, so thick, that total blindness could do no more; and how it is our duty therefore to trust not to the reasonings of interested men, or to their way of colouring a transaction... As soon as ever I had arrived thus far in my investigation of the slave trade, I confess to you sir, so enormous so dreadful, so irremediable did its wickedness appear that my own mind was completely made up for the abolition. A trade founded in iniquity, and carried on as this was, must be abolished, let the policy be what it might, – let the consequences be what they would, I from this time determined that I would never rest till I had effected its abolition.

Key:

= personal pronouns   = Emotive language

= Repetition   = Exclamatory sentence

= Use of three   = Rhetorical question

The main **devices** used in this persuasive speech are:
- **repetition**
- **emotive language**.

Repetition

The blue highlighted words and phrases in this speech are examples of **repetition**. Each repeated word or phrase is used to create a particular effect.

Personal pronouns

- Repeated use of the word *I*, as well as *my* and *me*, indicates a strong personal belief in and attachment to the subject.
- Use of *we* and *our* indicates that this is a shared vision and the speaker wants the audience to be a part of it, to support him, and to feel the way he does.

Sentence structure

- Repetition of sentence structures such as *when I...*, *I will...*, and *Let the...* add emphasis to the points the speaker makes.
- Groups of three are also used in the speech, i.e. where the same structure is used three times, for example, *so enormous, so dreadful, so irremediable*. This has the effect of helping to build up momentum or create emphasis.

Abolition

- The word *abolition* is repeated because it is the central theme of the speech.
- William Wilberforce believed that all people should have freedom and that the abolition of the slave trade was a hugely important and urgent issue.

Wretchedness

- Repetition of the word *wretchedness* and *wretched* emphasises the misery and wickedness of the slave trade.

Faith

- The power of this speech comes from the passionate belief that one day the slave trade will be abolished: *I from this time determined that I would never rest till I had effected its abolition*.
- William Wilberforce's **belief** and **perseverance** are central to this speech.

Key Point

Repetition helps to reinforce the main points of your speech, build up a rhythm and remind your audience of the main points.

Using repetition in your writing

If you are asked to write a speech about a topic you have strong feelings on, you should begin by **brainstorming**. Think about the important themes, key words, emotions and beliefs that you associate with that topic. These ideas will be the elements that you repeat in your speech.

Although **repetition** is the main device used in this speech, there are other devices that make it a powerful piece of writing.

Emotive language

William Wilberforce's speech has a very honest quality; there is no attempt to manipulate the reader or listener. **Emotive language** is used selectively throughout the speech to highlight certain points that the speaker makes.

- Sentences that contain emotive language, such as *it is impossible for me not to feel both terrified and concerned at my own inadequacy...* emphasise the speaker's feelings on the subject.
- Powerful emotive words like *horrid*, *misery*, *wretched*, *wickedness* and *evil* used throughout the speech help to convey the suffering and horror experienced.

Key Point	**Emotive language** is the use of words and phrases that evoke an emotional response.

Using emotive language in your writing

Think of some key **emotive** words or phrases you could use in your speech. Again, you could **brainstorm** your ideas and then select the most powerful and effective words to use in your final speech.

Think carefully about how you could best support the argument you are building. The following words could all be used to describe somebody's death: **died, killed, executed, slaughtered**. Each of these words indicates something different about the person and the circumstances of their death.

- **Died** – this is a neutral word.
- **Killed** – this suggests that somebody else is responsible for the death, but it is still quite a neutral word.
- **Executed** – this suggests that the person who is dead has been killed as a punishment for doing something wrong. This is quite an emotive word as it implies the person deserved to die according to certain value systems.
- **Slaughtered** – this is a very emotive word for two reasons. Firstly, it suggests a very violent and nasty death. Secondly, it implies that we should make a very different judgment about the person who is dead – they would probably be described as an innocent victim.

If you were writing a speech about the rights or wrongs of **capital punishment**, which of these words would you use?

Sentence structure

Look at the sentence structure of William Wilberforce's speech.

- The majority of the speech is made up of complex sentences, which build up pace, rhythm and momentum, as well as giving a detailed description of the issue and the speaker's thoughts on the issue.
- Use of three appears in the speech, for example, *...I take courage – I determine to forget all other my other fears, and I march forward....* Use of three is an effective technique, which is used to build up momentum and to highlight certain points.
- An exclamatory sentence is used, which adds to the sense of disbelief that such practices go on.
- This is followed by a rhetorical question which involves the audience by challenging them to allow such terrible scenes to continue. The use of *How can we bear...* suggests that no civilised person could stand to see it continue.
- The final sentence is a complex sentence, which contains the important ideas visited in the speech. It contains some repetition (*let the...*) and allows the speaker to end with a defiant tone.

Using sentence structure in your own writing

Think carefully about the **effects** you are trying to create. Try to use a variety of sentence structures and punctuation to change the pace and emphasis of your speech.

> ### Word level
>
> - Use the ending **-ssion** if there is a **short vowel** (**a**, **e** or **u**) before the **shun** sound: pa**ssion**, confe**ssion**.
> - Use the ending **-sion** if you can hear a **zhun** sound: persua**sion**. **Exceptions**: apprehen**sion**, comprehen**sion**, man**sion**, ten**sion**.

Progress Check

1. Put these words in order from most emotive to least emotive: *crowd, mob, gang*.
2. Think of a more emotive word to replace the highlighted word in the following headline: 'Train seats cut by teenage gang'.
3. Which of the following statements are true? Repetition is a useful device because a) it helps the reader or listener remember the important parts b) you don't need to think of as many points to make c) it builds up a rhythm.

1 Mob, gang, crowd   2 Slashed   3 a) and c)

8.3 Persuasive argument

Argument is a form of **persuasion**. If you have an argument with somebody, it is because you disagree about something. To win an argument, you must persuade your opponent that your point of view is correct.

A piece of persuasive argument writing is usually quite **formal**. Read the following example and think about the techniques that have been used to persuade the reader that the writer's point of view is correct.

Too much television can damage your child's health

Television may be part of everyday life for most children, but is it safe? In our hectic lives we are so busy managing our private and professional concerns and relationships, we allow our children to spend a huge percentage of their unsupervised time watching television. So busy, in fact, that most of us don't stop to consider the hidden dangers of unlimited viewing.

The health risks which attend excessive television viewing are extensive and, to my mind, should not be underestimated. It contributes to the growing problems of adolescent obesity; it prevents regular exercise, which could cause heart problems in later life; it causes psychological problems if children are exposed to inappropriate materials and it can damage eyesight.

However, the most worrying problem is the detrimental effect that too much television can have on the early stages of a child's development. Playing games, listening to stories and interacting with other children are all essential to a child's emotional, physical and communication development. When television takes the place of these activities, we allow untold damage to be done.

Of course, many would be quick to defend the educational value of television and there is no doubt that properly managed television viewing can be beneficial. In my opinion, however, the dangers far outweigh the benefits. Until parents make time to exercise proper control over their children's viewing habits, children's health will continue to suffer.

How does the text work?

Title

- The title is an opinion presented as a fact. This type of sentence is a **statement**; this gives the writer's opinion authority.
- The statement is shocking and it captures the reader's attention and interest immediately.
- The topic of this piece of argument is immediately obvious.

Structure

The argument is organised into four paragraphs:

1. an introduction setting up the main point of the argument and offering a challenging point of view
2. a range of reasons is given to support the writer's point of view
3. the most important supporting reason is given a paragraph of its own for emphasis
4. the final paragraph concludes the argument by anticipating a possible counter-argument.

AF2
You should be able to present a case persuasively, making selective use of evidence, using appropriate rhetorical devices and anticipating responses and objections.

Connectives

The writer uses a range of logical connectives to keep the text varied and interesting:

- *to my mind*
- *however*
- *of course*
- *in my opinion*
- *but*.

Repetition

The second paragraph uses repetition effectively. Each reason why television is damaging is introduced in the same way: *it prevents regular exercise; it causes . . . .*

Sentence structure

This is a **formal** piece of writing aimed at an **adult audience**. Most sentences are complex and employ a range of punctuation.

Sentence level

The language choices we make at **word**, **sentence** and **text level** vary according to audience, purpose, topic and context. Most people make a range of quite sophisticated choices about language, to change the formality of their writing or speech, without even thinking about it.

Key Point Persuasive argument uses the same devices that have been discussed in topics 8.1 and 8.2.

Writing your own persuasive argument

Plan

First you will need to plan the main points of your argument. The following table shows the points for and against school uniform. Each point '**against**' could be the main point of a paragraph in your argument. You could use the '**for**' points to anticipate and answer any counter-arguments.

School uniform	
For	**Against**
Sense of school identity	Uncomfortable
Smart	Expensive
Easy to identify on trips and visits	Unfashionable
Saves other clothes from wear and	Impractical for some subjects
tear and subject-related damage,	Prevents expression of personality
e.g. art, science	Creates petty discipline problems

Before you begin, you should decide on the best **order** for these points. Think about how you can **link** the different strands of your argument together.

A persuasive introduction

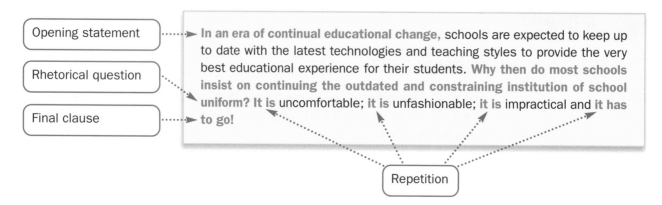

Opening statement

Rhetorical question

Final clause

In an era of continual educational change, schools are expected to keep up to date with the latest technologies and teaching styles to provide the very best educational experience for their students. **Why then do most schools insist on continuing the outdated and constraining institution of school uniform? It is** uncomfortable; **it is** unfashionable; **it is** impractical and **it has to go!**

Repetition

- **Opening statement** – establishes the idea of change.
- **Rhetorical question** – used for emphasis to show that in this area there has been little change.
- **Repetition** – also used for emphasis; each clause in the sentence has the same structure.
- **Final clause** – the change from *it is* to *it has to* adds further emphasis to the final point

Linking the points in your argument

Use a range of connectives, such as:
- **furthermore**
- **another reason for this**
- **not only**
- **on the other hand**
- **despite the fact that**
- **however**
- **nevertheless**.

The following sentence is an **effective link** because it looks back to the previous paragraph of the argument and sets up the next main point:

> Not only is school uniform unfashionable and embarrassing, it is also extremely uncomfortable and impractical.

Anticipating opposition and counter-argument

Try to use **opposing** views to strengthen your own case. If you express **counter-arguments**, you can make them appear weaker than your own. For example:

> Many people contend that school uniform helps to create a sense of school identity and helps students feel that they belong. What other institutions require their members to wear a uniform? Prison is the first example that springs to mind! In prison, inmates lose the freedom to express themselves. School uniform imprisons the wearer, taking away the freedom to express personality and individuality. If schools want to create a sense of identity: why not let students create that identity themselves?

Using evidence to support your argument

If you have **facts or data** to back up your argument, think carefully about how you use them. For example:
- **51%** is better expressed as **over 50%**
- **1 in 8** sounds more impressive than **12%**.

Sentence structure

In **formal** argument you will need to use longer complex sentences in order to express a range of complex ideas. However, controlled use of short, simple sentences for emphasis will make your writing more powerful.

> ### Word level
>
> The example introduction on page 120 uses several prefixes: *uncomfortable*, *unfashionable*, and *impractical*.
>
> A **prefix** is a group of letters added to the beginning of a **root word** to change its meaning. In most cases, adding a prefix does not change the spelling of the root word, even if this means **doubling a consonant** at the beginning of the root word: necessary → **un**necessary; satisfied → **dis**satisfied.

8.4 Discursive argument

Discursive writing is sometimes called a **balanced argument** because it looks at both sides of the argument, giving each equal weight.
Writing in this style includes:

- **magazine or newspaper articles** that consider all angles of an argument
- **formal essays** that compare and contrast or discuss advantages and disadvantages.

A discursive text

Opening statement

Introduction of evidence

Use of logical connectives

Rhetorical question

Linking phrase

Arguments presented without bias

Many schools in the United Kingdom are beginning to explore the benefits of a more flexible day. Research has shown that children study more effectively during the morning and therefore, some schools are opening their doors earlier to teach more lessons before lunch, leaving the afternoons free for sport and extra-curricular activities. **However,** many parents oppose the new continental-style day as it interferes with childcare arrangements and means that some children could be left roaming the streets after school has finished.

So what are the benefits? Head teacher, Alan Brown, claims that since changing the structure of the school day, students in all years have achieved greater exam success and there has been a significant reduction in low-level disruption to lessons. His claims are supported by a 5% increase in A*–C grade GCSE passes since the changes were introduced.

However, despite the apparent success of the continental day at Mr Brown's school, critics have warned that it is too early to attribute exam success to the new school day. Many parents believe that the increased workload during the morning session means that students are being expected to work for too long without a proper break. Some students who live 30 minutes away from the school have to wait from 7.30 a.m. until 1.30 p.m. before they have the chance to eat anything. **Opponents** of the changes claim that lack of rest and nourishment will have a negative effect on examination results in the next few years.

The conventions of a discursive text

- **Opening statement** – this introduces the topic to be discussed.
- *Research has shown* – **connective phrases** are used to introduce evidence.
- **Logical connectives** – phrases such as **therefore, however, despite this, as a result** are used regularly.
- **Rhetorical questions** – are used to introduce argument and counter-argument rather than for persuasive emphasis.
- **Linking phrases** – are used to link paragraphs of argument and counter-argument.
- **Arguments presented without bias** – discursive writing presents the opinions of others, but gives both sides equal weighting. The writer does not give his or her opinion in the main body of the text. The views

expressed in the text are credited to specific people or groups of people, distancing them from the writer or 'narrator'. The writer may sometimes express an opinion favouring the argument or counter-argument in the conclusion.

- **Voice and tense** – discursive writing uses the **present tense** and the **third person**. The first person is sometimes used in the conclusion.
- **Structure** – each paragraph or section explores a main point of the argument, followed by the opposing point from the counter-argument.

Using Standard English – formality

This kind of writing requires a **formal style** and you must avoid non-standard forms, as they are inappropriate in argument writing. The following non-standard forms should be avoided.

- Using **adjectives** as **adverbs**:
  She won **easy**. ✗
  She won **easily**. ✔
- Mixing **singular** and **plural** in subject / verb agreement:
  He **were** frightened. ✗
  He **was** frightened. ✔
  We **was** bad. ✗
  We **were** bad. ✔
- Using '**them**' as a **determiner**:
  I bought **them** oranges. ✗
  I bought **those** oranges. ✔
- Using '**what**' as a **relative pronoun**:
  Have you seen the book **what** I bought? ✗
  Have you seen the book **that** I bought? ✔

The highlighted terms are explained in Chapter 11.

Progress Check

1. A discursive argument looks at all sides of an issue. TRUE or FALSE?
2. When can you give your own opinion in a discursive essay: introduction / main text / conclusion?
3. Change the highlighted non-standard forms in the following sentence: 'We **was** hoping to give you a **real** good present this year.'

1 True 2 Conclusion 3 Were, really

Have a go

Write a paragraph of argument and counter-argument for the following points about the 'continental school day':

- **Argument** – students can take part in more sport, drama and extra-curricular activities.
- **Counter-argument** – schools can't force students to stay for these activities, so they could be roaming the streets from 2 p.m.

Assessment questions

The following questions will help you to prepare for the **Optional Tests** and **APP tasks**.

1. Write two or three paragraphs to **persuade** the reader of the need for better leisure facilities in your area.

2. Write four paragraphs of **discursive writing** discussing the advantages and disadvantages of teenagers having mobile phones.

3. Imagine you are the director of a new museum.

    Write a letter to head teachers of schools in the area **persuading** them to bring groups of pupils to the museum.

    You could write about:
    *   what the museum has to offer
    *   why it is of educational value
    *   how to organise a trip there.

4. Imagine you have been given a chance to give a talk to your class. Choose an issue you feel strongly about.

    Write a talk trying to **persuade** other people to support your views.

5. Write a **discursive essay** about keeping animals in zoos and safari parks.

    Write about:
    *   points **for** keeping animals in captivity
    *   points **against** keeping animals in captivity
    *   your own opinion.

The Writing Papers of the Optional Tests will assess your responses across all of the Assessment Focuses for Writing (listed on page 157). Your teacher may use APP to assess one or more of the Assessment Focuses in your ongoing work or in specific tasks. If you have been set a specific task, your teacher will usually tell you which Assessment Focuses will be targeted.

When you attempt the questions on this page you should decide whether to concentrate on an Assessment Focus you know you need to improve on or whether to test your skills across all of the AFs.

9 Writing to review, analyse and comment

After studying this section you should be able to:

- **write a review**
- **provide analysis and comment on a piece of writing**

To achieve the following National Curriculum levels you need to do the following for each level.

Level 4
- **Organise** your writing in an **informative** and **interesting** way.
- **Comment** on the **plot** and **characters** in fiction and **main stylistic features of non-fiction**.

Level 5
- Use a **formal style** where appropriate.
- Select **relevant textual evidence** to support your comments.

Level 6
- Comment on the **significance** and **effect of layers of meaning** in a text.
- **Justify your views** by referring to language, structure and themes.

Level 7
- Give a **personal** and **critical** response to a range of literary texts.
- Use an appropriately **formal style** while still **engaging the interest of the reader**.

9.1 Writing reviews

When you write a **review** of something you are giving your **own opinion**. This could be completely different from somebody else's opinion on the same topic. You might be asked to write a review about:

- a **book**
- a **film**
- a **television programme**
- an **exhibition**
- a **play**.

What to include

Although a review is made up largely of your **opinion**, you will probably need to provide the reader with some **facts and information**, such as:

- the **title and author / director**, etc.
- a **summary** of the story
- **information** about the exhibition
- **where** you can buy the book or see the film / exhibition / play.

The **audience** of a written review will usually be people who want to know if they would enjoy the book, film, play or exhibition. You should include your opinions on:

- its **strengths**
- its **weaknesses**
- its **suitability** for a particular audience.

A review of *Kit's Wilderness*

The following extract includes information about the novel *Kit's Wilderness* and discusses its strengths. Notice how the information about the storyline **indicates the writer's opinion** of the book. If he or she thought the story was boring it would have been described in a very different way.

> Whitbread-winning author, David Almond's book *Kit's Wilderness* is about the place where magic and dreams collide with everyday life. Having moved back to the village of Stoneygate, Kit Watson finds himself drawn into John Askew's magical and frightening world. He meets Askew in the wilderness where he must confront life and death.
>
> Almond's writing is elegant and powerful. He manages to speak volumes with the things he doesn't say, while entrancing his readers with what he does. *Kit's Wilderness* is filled with suspense, mystery and wonder. His characters are real, his situations believable and his conclusions satisfying. In fact, *Kit's Wilderness* satisfies on every level.

9.2 Analysis and comment

The **reading** chapters of this study guide (**Chapters 2 to 4**) demonstrate an **analytical style** of writing. Whenever you are asked to write about something you have read, you will be required to comment on or analyse the language, structure or themes of the text. This style of writing is usually very **formal**.

Writing style

The **conventions** of analytical writing are:

- it's written in the **third person**
- **opinions are expressed in a detached way** – avoid phrases such as 'I think that. . .'
- opinions are **supported by textual evidence**
- non-standard forms and colloquial expression should be avoided.

Key Point

Analysis and comment writing is usually a response to a specific question, e.g. **Comment on the use of imagery in Wilfred Owen's poem 'Dulce et Decorum Est'**.

Structure

An **analytical essay** should follow a set pattern.

- **Introduction** – this should refer to key words in the question, capture the attention of the reader and demonstrate an understanding of the question.
- **Series of paragraphs** – these will explore different aspects of the question. Paragraphs should be linked and main points should be supported with quotation.
- **Conclusion** – this should refer back to the main points of your analysis and give your personal response to the question.

Paragraph structure

A useful way to structure your analysis in each paragraph is:

- make a **statement** or **point**
- use **quotation** or **textual evidence** to back up your statement
- **explain** your comment with **reference** to the evidence you have cited.

This is often called the 'PEE' rule – Point, Evidence, Explanation – or 'PEC' rule – Point, Evidence, Comment.

Below is an analysis of Macbeth's soliloquy discussed in **Chapter 2**.

Point

Explanation / Comment

Throughout this soliloquy, Macbeth uses euphemisms for the murder of Duncan: 'bear the knife', 'his taking-off', 'horrid deed'. Shakespeare has used this kind of language to demonstrate that Macbeth is reluctant to think about the brutality of the act of murder. He is trying to avoid the reality of the situation and cannot face up to the evil nature of the plan that he and his wife have made.

Quotation / Evidence

Presenting textual evidence

The following examples show how quotations should be set out in your writing.

- **Single words** and **short phrases** should be used as part of the sentence you are writing. The words you are quoting should be placed inside **quotation marks** (inverted commas or speech marks). The rules of punctuation are similar to speech punctuation.

In the first poem Blake's description of the beadles is positive. They are referred to as *wise*, suggesting they will know how to look after the children. The word *guardian* suggests protection. They are also described as carrying *wands as white as snow* – this simile makes the reader think of innocence and purity.

- **Longer quotations of whole sentences or lines of poetry** should be presented on a line of their own. Lines of quotation should be slightly **indented** and do not need quotation marks.

Owen uses two similes to show how tired and ill the soldiers are:

> Bent double, like old beggars under sacks,
> Knock-kneed, coughing like hags, we cursed through sludge,

These images are very direct and unpleasant and immediately show that Owen does not believe the sentiment expressed in the title of his poem. During the war, people wanted to imagine brave, healthy soldiers fighting for their country. Owen shows that, although they may have joined the army in that state, the war has damaged them beyond repair.

Progress Check

1. A book review should contain the opinions of the reviewer. TRUE or FALSE?
2. Short phrase quotations should be presented on a line of their own. TRUE or FALSE?
3. Quotations that are presented on a line of their own do not need quotation marks. TRUE or FALSE?

1 True   2 False   3 True

Assessment questions

The following questions will help you to prepare for the **Optional Tests** and **APP tasks**.

1. Write a review of the last fiction book you read. You should refer to the strengths and weaknesses of the book.

2. Write a review of a film or television drama you have watched recently, giving your recommendations about who should watch it.

3. Watch two television advertisements for similar products. Write an analysis of the effectiveness of the techniques used to persuade the target audience.
   Think about:
   - the audience and purpose
   - use of music and / or special effects
   - use of different camera angles.

4. Write a relationship study on two main characters in a novel you have read recently.
   Comment on:
   - how the characters are presented to the reader
   - how the relationship changes
   - how effectively the author conveys this relationship.

The Writing Papers of the Optional Tests will assess your responses across all of the Assessment Focuses for Writing (listed on page 157). Your teacher may use APP to assess one or more of the Assessment Focuses in your ongoing work or in specific tasks. If you have been set a specific task, your teacher will usually tell you which Assessment Focuses will be targeted.

When you attempt the questions on this page you should decide whether to concentrate on an Assessment Focus you know you need to improve on or whether to test your skills across all of the AFs.

10 Spelling

After studying this section you should be able to:

- **use spelling strategies effectively**
- **understand spelling rules**
- **understand and use prefixes and suffixes**
- **use and spell homophones correctly**

To achieve the following National Curriculum levels you need to do the following for each level.

Level 4
- Spell **basic words** and **polysyllabic words** (words with more than one syllable) that fit into regular patterns correctly.

Level 5
- Spell words with **complex regular** patterns correctly.

Level 6
- Ensure that spelling, including **irregular** words, is usually accurate.

Level 7
- Ensure that spelling is always correct, including **complex irregular** words.

10.1 Spelling strategies

The best ways to improve your spelling are to:
- **learn spelling rules**
- **learn commonly misspelt words**
- **practise spelling strategies.**

Look – Say – Cover – Write – Check

- **Look** at the word you want to learn: try to find patterns; learn the shape of the word.

- **Say** the word.

- **Cover** the word with your hand and **write** it down.

- **Check** your spelling. If you made a mistake, go back to the beginning and look carefully at the part of the word you got wrong.

Use a dictionary

AF8
You should be able to:
* make effective use of a **spellchecker**, recognising where it might not be sufficient or appropriate;
* use a **dictionary** and a **thesaurus** with speed and skill.

Use a **dictionary** to check the spelling of words you are unsure of. Many dictionaries will also give you **information** about the **roots** and **origins** of words; this is sometimes helpful in learning a new spelling.

You could also use an **electronic spellchecker** or the spellchecker facility on your computer. If you use your computer, make sure it has a UK English checker. Remember that some of the words you use may not be recognised by the computer, particularly names, but this does not mean the spelling is incorrect.

You can't use a dictionary or electronic spellchecker in any kind of English exam, so **make sure you use all of the other strategies for learning spellings too**.

Mnemonics

AF8
You should be able to identify words which pose a challenge and learn them by using **mnemonics** and memorising critical features.

Some people find spellings easier to remember if they make up a rhyme to go with them, for example:

Rhythm **h**as **y**our **t**wo **h**ands **m**oving → Rhythm

Big **e**lephants **c**an't **a**lways **u**se **s**mall **e**xits → Because

Say the word as it is spelt

AF8
You should be able to **sound out words** phonemically (each sound in a word) and by syllables.

Words that have **silent letters** or **unstressed syllables** in them are often easier to remember if you sound the part of the word that is usually silent. For example:
* We**d**nesday
* lis**t**en
* pe**o**ple.

Break words into parts

Polysyllabic words can be broken into smaller chunks to make them easier to remember. It is almost impossible to spell a word completely incorrectly. Work out which part of a word you find difficult and learn it, for example:

Ex – plan – a – tion

Make a spelling journal

AF8
You should be able to recognise and record personal errors, corrections, investigations, conventions, exceptions and new vocabulary.

Making a spelling journal will help you to learn spellings you find difficult.
- **Make a record** of all the words you find difficult to spell.
- Get a **list of key words** for each of your school subjects.
- Record some of the **spelling rules** you find helpful and refer to them when you are trying to spell a word you are unsure of.
- **Investigate spelling patterns** and have a go at difficult spellings before asking for help.

10.2 Spelling rules

Plurals

The following rules will help you with your spelling. However, you need to look out for the **exceptions** to these rules. Unfortunately, there are quite a lot of them!

There are some examples for you to try with each rule.

Adding -s and -es

RULE: To make a word into a plural add -s

    school → school**s**   shoe → shoe**s**   book → book**s**

If a word ends in -ss, -sh, -ch, -x, -zz add -es

    lunch → lunch**es**   glass → glass**es**   box → box**es**

HINT! Words that end in a **hissing**, **shushing** or **buzzing** sound add **-es**. When you say **-es** plurals aloud you can hear an extra syllable.

Exceptions

The other rules and conventions below show the exceptions to the simple plural rule.

Words that end in -y

RULE: If a word ends in a vowel followed by **-y**, you add **-s**. If a word ends in a consonant followed by **-y**, you change the **-y** to **-i** and add **-es**.

toy ➜ toy**s**   key ➜ key**s**   try ➜ tr**ies**   factory ➜ factor**ies**

Progress Check

1. Add -s or -es to make the following words plural:
   bench, fox, church, pupil, light, wish, wash
2. Add -s or change the ending to make the following words plural:
   boy, fly, monkey, play, baby, lady, bay

1 benches, foxes, churches, pupils, lights, wishes, washes
2 boys, flies, monkeys, plays, babies, ladies, bays

Key Point

The rules for words ending in **-f** and **-y** apply when you are adding any other ending.

Words that end in -f, -ff and -fe

Any words that end in **-ff** need an **-s** to make them plural, for example:

sheriff ➜ sheriff**s**   cuff ➜ cuff**s**

Words that end in **-f** or **-fe** are more difficult. Some are made plural by adding **-s**, such as:

chief ➜ chief**s**   reef ➜ reef**s**

Other words change the **-f** to **-v** and add **-es**, such as:

wife ➜ wi**ves**   leaf ➜ lea**ves**   calf ➜ cal**ves**

Some words that end in **-f** can be spelt with either an **-fs** or a **-ves** plural ending, such as:

scarf ➜ scar**fs** or scar**ves**   hoof ➜ hoo**fs** or hoo**ves**

HINT! As there is no clear rule, **a tip that often works is saying the plural aloud**. If you can hear a **v** sound then it usually means the correct spelling is **-ves**.

cli**ffs** = **f** sound   cal**ves** = **v** sound

Irregular plurals

Some plural forms don't seem to follow any of these rules and the whole word changes, such as:

mouse ➜ **mice**   child ➜ **children**

You need to learn these words as you meet them.

Words that end in -o

Words that end in **-o** or **-oo** don't follow set patterns. Try to group words together as you learn them.

tomato	potato	mango – all edible and all end in **-es**
tomato**es**	potato**es**	mango**es**
toma**toes**	pota**toes**	mosqui**toes** – they all have **toes** in them

No change plurals

Some words don't change at all! You need to learn these:

sheep   deer   fish

Key Point

Foreign words follow different rules. Learn them as you need them, e.g. cactus → cacti, fungus → fungi.

Progress Check

1. Add **-s** or change the ending to make the following words plural: wolf, knife, life, loaf, roof
2. What are the plural forms of the following? man, woman, goose, foot
3. What are the plural forms of the following? Use a dictionary if you need to. radio, volcano, shampoo, go

1 wolves, knives, lives, loaves, roofs 2 men, women, geese, feet 3 radios, volcanoes, shampoos, goes

---

10.3 Prefixes and suffixes

Prefixes

AF8
You should be familiar with spelling rules for **word endings**, including **vowel suffixes** such as -ing; **consonant suffixes** such as -ful; **prefixes**.

A **prefix** is a group of two or three letters added to the beginning of a word to change or qualify the meaning, e.g. **dis-, mis-, pre-, un-**.

Rule

When you add a prefix you **do not** change the spelling of the original word:
satisfied → **dis**satisfied
spelling → **mis**spelling
necessary → **un**necessary

Key Point

Remember, prefixes **never** change the root word.

Suffixes

A **suffix** is a group of two or three letters added to the end of a word to make a derivative of the original, e.g. **-ed**, **-ful**, **-ing**, **-ly**, **-ment**. Sometimes adding a suffix changes the spelling of the original word.

Rules

Adding a vowel suffix -ed, -ing and -y
If the word has one syllable, one short vowel and ends in a single consonant, you **double the consonant** when you add the ending:

stop ➜ sto**pp**ed ➜ sto**pp**ing

fit ➜ fi**tt**ed ➜ fi**tt**ing

mud ➜ mu**dd**y

Words with more than one syllable or vowel and words that end with a double consonant, take the suffix **without changing the root**:

boss ➜ boss**y**

deliver ➜ deliver**y**

focus ➜ focus**ing**

groom ➜ groom**ed**

If the word ends in -e you only add the -d of -ed. You omit the -e if you are adding -ing or able:

continu**e** – continu**ed**

mak**e** – mak**ing**

excit**e** – excit**able**

Adding a consonant suffix
In most cases, the root word does not change when you add a suffix that begins with a consonant. Remember the following points.

Adding -ful
RULE: Remember, full becomes -ful. You do not change the original word unless it ends in y (see y ending rule).

fit ➜ fit**ful**

hope ➜ hope**ful**

Adding -ly
RULE: The original word does not change when you add -ly.

real ➜ real**ly**

proper ➜ proper**ly**

careful ➜ careful**ly**

Words that end in **-le** don't follow the same rule. For these words, miss out the final **-e** and add **-y**.

responsib**le** ➜ responsib**ly**

possib**le** ➜ possib**ly**

Words ending in -y or -f

The rules for adding suffixes to words ending in **-y** or **-f** are the same as the pluralising rules.

fry ➜ fr**ied**

beauty ➜ beaut**iful**

happy ➜ happ**ily**

play ➜ play**ed**

shelf ➜ shel**ving**

Progress Check

How many words can you make from these prefixes and suffixes?

Prefix	Root	Suffix
mis	appoint	ment
pre	fortunate	ful
dis	view	ly
un	event	ed
	understand	ing

misunderstand, misunderstanding, understanding, understandingly, preview, previewed, previewing, viewed, viewing, disappoint, disappointment, disappointingly, disappointing, disappointed, appointment, appointed, appointing, uneventful, uneventfully, eventfully, eventful, unfortunate, unfortunately, fortunately

---

Key Point

Learning **prefix** and **suffix** rules will help you to spell polysyllabic words.

10.4 Homophones and commonly misspelt words

Homophones

AF8
You should be familiar with the spellings of high-frequency words including common homophones.

There are many words in the English language that sound the same but are spelt differently and have different meanings. They are known as **homophones**.

Many of these are basic words that are commonly used in everyday writing. Look at the table opposite for details of some of the most common homophones. You must learn the spellings of these words.

ARE	present form of the verb **to be: Where** *are* **you going? We** *are* **all the same age.**	
OUR	belonging to us: **We're going to** *our* **house.**	
HEAR	to perceive sound: **Can you** *hear* **me?**	
HERE	referring to place: **Come over** *here*.	
THEIR	belonging to them: **We're going to** *their* **house.**	
THERE	referring to place: **It's over** *there*. indicating the fact or existence of something: *There* **is a horse in the field.**	
THEY'RE	short form of **they are:** *They're* **coming to our house.**	
THREW	past tense of throw: **He** *threw* **the ball.**	
THROUGH	**He went** *through* **the door. I read the letter** *through*, **from beginning to end.**	
TO	introduces a noun or a verb: **Are you going** *to* **school? I was going** *to* **walk today.**	Noun / Verb
TOO	also / as well: **Can we come** *too*? excessive: **It was** *too* **hot. That is** *too* **expensive.**	
TWO	the number 2: **I ate** *two* **pieces of cake.**	
SAW	past tense of see: **I** *saw* **you taking it.** tool and action to cut wood: **Pass me the** *saw*. **I will** *saw* **the plank in half.**	
SOAR	to fly or rise high: **Eagles can** *soar* **high in the sky.**	
SORE	painful: **My leg was** *sore*.	
WEAR	of clothes, etc.: **I** *wear* **school uniform.**	
WERE	past tense of **are: We** *are* **going to school. / We** *were* **going to school.**	
WE'RE	short form of **we are:** *We're* **going to school.**	
WHERE	referring to place: *Where* **is it?**	
WHO'S	short form of **who is:** *Who's* **going to be captain?**	
WHOSE	belonging to: *Whose* **bag is this?**	

Strategies for learning homophones

The best way to ensure that you use homophones correctly is to learn them. Some ideas that might help you to learn them are:
- **look for patterns**
- **make groups of words** that have similar spellings or meanings
- **draw pictures or cartoons**
- **make up rhymes.**

Key Point	• The word 'there' has many different uses. 'Their' and 'they're' have only one use each. Learn the use of **their** and **they're** first; **there** is used on all other occasions. • Here, there and where are all place words.

Commonly misspelt words

The following words are often spelt incorrectly. It is a good idea to learn them as they sometimes fail to fit into normal spelling patterns. The parts of the words that cause confusion or difficulty have been highlighted.

acceptable	use **able** if the rest of the word will stand alone – **accept**	necessary	never eat cake eat salad sandwiches and remain young
accommodation			one collar and two socks
achieve	i before e except after c	permanent	
analyse		persuade	
assess		physical	
believe	i before e except after c	receive	i before e except after c
communicate		recommend	
convenient	i before e except after c	responsible	
definite		separate	there's a rat in separate
desperate		stationary	not moving
disappear	root words never change when you add a prefix	stationery	paper, etc.
		success	
disappoint	root words never change when you add a prefix	surprise	
		weird	a weird exception to the rule! (i before e except after c)

Key Point	Don't forget to use LOOK, SAY, COVER, WRITE, CHECK to learn these words.

11 Punctuation and grammar

After studying this section you should be able to:

- **use punctuation marks effectively**
- **use speech punctuation effectively**
- **use apostrophes correctly**
- **structure text using paragraphs**
- **recognise and use sentence types**
- **recognise and use parts of speech**

To achieve the following National Curriculum levels you need to do the following for each level.

Level 4

- Use **full stops, capital letters** and **question marks** accurately.
- Use **commas** in lists.
- Begin to use **complex sentences**.

Level 5

- Use **commas** to mark clauses.
- Use **apostrophes** and **speech punctuation** correctly.
- Clearly **structure** your writing **using paragraphs**.
- Use a **wide range of vocabulary**.

Level 6

- Use **punctuation** to develop **a range of complex sentences**.
- Use **punctuation** to **clarify meaning**.

Level 7

- Show **increasing control of a range of sentence types**.
- Use **punctuation** to **clarify meaning and create effects**.

Key Point	Grammar is the way we organise words to make sense: • 'This is my dog' is grammatical and it makes sense. • 'My this is dog' is ungrammatical – it makes no sense at all.

11.1 Punctuation marks

When we talk, we use different tones of voice and pause after certain words to make our meaning clear. When we write, we use **punctuation** to make our meaning clear.

Capital letters and full stops

Capital letters and **full stops** show where a sentence begins and ends:
the cat was sick in the morning we decided to take it to the vet
The cat was sick. In the morning we decided to take it to the vet.

Capital letters are also used for:
- the word 'I'
- initials – **BBC**, **RAC**
- names of people, places and products, e.g. **Jane**, **Brazil**, **Weetabix**.

Commas

Commas help us to understand the meaning within a sentence. They are used to:

- **separate items in a list**
You will need a pen, a pencil, a ruler and a rubber.
- **separate additional information (embedded clauses) from the rest of the sentence**

John, who was very angry, shouted at the children.

- **separate subordinate clauses from main clauses**

Subordinate ········► When the rope snapped, the climber fell and broke his leg. Main

- **after** the following words: however, therefore, of course, nevertheless.

Colons and semicolons

Colons are advanced punctuation marks. They point ahead to something which follows; this could be a quotation in an essay or the beginning of a list.

The **semicolon** is another advanced punctuation mark. It is used to join two sentences that are very closely linked; this may be where a full stop seems too strong and a comma too weak.

Semicolons are also used to separate items in a list when they are phrases rather than single words:

Before you go out you should: tidy your bedroom; wash the dishes; feed the cat and hang the washing out.

11.2 Speech punctuation

Speech marks

Speech marks are essential in your writing to show clearly that someone has spoken. Speech marks are generally used correctly, but there is a lot more to punctuating speech than just speech marks. Here are some basic rules to follow.

Rules

- Speech marks "..." or '...' are placed **around the words a person actually speaks**.
- The first word inside the speech marks always begins with a **capital letter**.
- The words inside speech marks always end with a **mark of punctuation** (full stop, comma, question mark or exclamation mark).
- If the sentence is continued after the speech marks (with 'he said', etc.), then you don't end the speech with a full stop, and the first word outside the speech marks must begin with a small letter:

  'Tidy your bedroom before you go out,' said my mother.

- If the sentence begins with 'he said', a comma must follow this before you open the speech marks:

  The man turned and whispered, 'Never ask me that again.'

- When a new speaker begins, you must begin a **new paragraph**.

Progress Check

Add the correct punctuation to these sentences.
1. shut up shouted james you don't know what you're talking about
2. i want to go home now mum whispered the bored child
3. i saw james the boy who broke his leg on the bbc news last night
4. when the bell rang the teacher dismissed the class

1. 'Shut up!' shouted James, 'You don't know what you're talking about.'
2. 'I want to go home now mum,' whispered the bored child.
3. I saw James, the boy who broke his leg, on the BBC news last night.
4. When the bell rang, the teacher dismissed the class.

11.3 Apostrophes

There are two ways to use **apostrophes**:
- to indicate **omission**
- to indicate **possession**.

Apostrophes – omission

Apostrophes are used to show that a letter, or letters, have been missed out when writing a short form. For example: **cannot** becomes **can't**.

If you remember **why** apostrophes are used then you should always get them in the right place.

People often think that the apostrophe goes between the two words that are being joined; this is wrong.

> **does + not = does'nt ✗**
>
> **does + not = doesn't ✔**
>
> **you + will = you'll ✔**

Apostrophes – possession

Apostrophes are used to show that something belongs to someone or something:

> **Iqbal's bag – the bag belonging to Iqbal.**

- When something belongs to a single person or thing, add apostrophe and s:
  the cat's whiskers; Sally's coat; the boy's homework.
- If the word already ends in s, then just add an apostrophe after the s:
  James' book.
- When something belongs to more than one person or thing, add an apostrophe after the s:
  the cats' whiskers; the girls' bags; ladies' coats.
- If the plural form of a word does not end in s, then add an apostrophe and s:
  the children's homework; the men's hats.
- It is not just objects that belong to people: emotions, people and actions also belong:
  Sunita's anger; Amanda's fear; Leroy's father; the poet's writing.
- 'Belonging to it' does not follow the above rules:
  its = belonging to it
  it's = it is.

Progress Check

1. Write out the short forms of these words using apostrophes:
   do not, they will, have not, I am, would not.
2. Add the possessive apostrophes to the phrases below.
   the mans strength, the girls bags (singular), the girls bags (plural), yesterdays meeting, Lauras ambition

2 man's, girl's, girls', yesterday's, Laura's
1 don't, they'll, haven't, I'm, wouldn't

11.4 Paragraphs

- A paragraph is a **group of sentences** linked to the same topic.
- Paragraphs help you to **organise** your work.
- In handwriting, indicate paragraphs by **starting a new line and indenting 1cm from the margin**.

Organising your writing into paragraphs

There are three ways to organise paragraphs:
- by **time**
- by **topic**
- by **talk**.

Look at this extract from *A Kestrel for a Knave*. Notice how the paragraphs are organised.

Topic — Billy tried another rush. Sugden repelled it, so he tried the other end again. Every time he tried to escape the three boys bounced him back, stinging him with their snapping towels as he retreated. . ..

Time — When Billy stopped yelling the other boys stopped laughing, and when time passed and no more was heard from him, their conversations began to peter out, and attention gradually focused on the showers. . ..

Topic — The boy guards began to look uneasy, and they looked across to their captain.

Talk — 'Can we let him out now, Sir?'
'No!'

11.5 Sentences

There are three types of sentence:
- **simple**
- **compound**
- **complex**.

These sentence types fall into four categories:
- **statements** – The boy laughed. (declarative)
- **questions** – Did you hear me? (interrogative)
- **commands** – Come here now. (imperative)
- **exclamations** – What a mess! (exclamatory)

Simple sentences

A sentence usually contains a **subject** and a **verb**.

Subject

My sister runs in the park.

Verb

Phrase (in this case information about where it happens)

Simple sentences give you one main piece of information.

I ran home. I was late. My mum was angry.

| Key Point | If you want to achieve **Level 5** and above you need to use a range of sentences – simple, compound and complex. |

Compound sentences

Compound sentences are made up from simple sentences or clauses joined together by conjunctions: **and**, **but** and **or**. All the clauses have equal weight, as they are all main clauses.

I ran home. I was late and my mum was angry but she didn't tell me off.

| Key Point | A **clause** must contain a **subject** and a **verb**. |

Complex sentences

Complex sentences are made up of two or more clauses, **one of which must be a subordinate clause**. A **clause** has a **subject** and contains a **verb**.

| Key Point | • A **main clause** can stand alone as a sentence: **I was cold**.
• A **subordinate clause** does not make sense alone. It relies on the main clause for its meaning: **because I had forgotten my coat**

I was cold because I had forgotten my coat. |

Subordinate clauses

AF5

Subordinate clauses give background information, for example: when something happened or how people feel. They help you to create two-part sentences. Subordinate clauses can be used in the first or second half of a sentence; sometimes they can be embedded.

The subordinate clause in each of the sentences below has been underlined.

Subordinate clauses begin with:

• a **subordinating conjunction** – **although**, **however**, **because**:

    <u>Although</u> her feet hurt, Jane carried on running.

• a **relative pronoun** – **who**, **which**, **whose**, **that**. This kind of subordinate clause is known as a **relative clause**. You cannot begin a sentence with a **relative clause**:

    My shoes, <u>which are old and smelly,</u> need to be thrown away.
    I hoped <u>that he would enjoy the match.</u>
    I can see the man <u>whose car was stolen.</u>

AF5

You should be able to:
- recognise and use **subordinate clauses**
- explore the function of subordinate clauses
- use subordinate clauses in a variety of positions in a sentence.

- a non-finite verb (see **11.6 Parts of speech** for more detail). The non-finite verb form is particularly useful as it allows you to manipulate your sentences and move the subordinate clause around. A non-finite verb can be placed before or after the noun:

> Filled with despair, the football manager left the pitch. (**beginning**)
> The football manager, filled with despair, left the pitch. (**embedded**)
> The football manager left the pitch, filled with despair. (**end**)

Embedded clauses

An **embedded clause** is a subordinate clause that is placed in the middle of a main clause – a bit like a bracketed aside giving extra information.

- The teacher shouted at the children. (**simple sentence**)
- The teacher shouted at the children because he was angry. (**subordinate clause at the end**)
- The teacher, who was filled with anger, shouted at the children. (**embedded subordinate clause**)

Key Point

It is important to use a range of sentences in your writing. This will allow you to create rhythm and interest in your writing.

Progress Check

1. A subordinate clause can stand as a sentence alone. TRUE or FALSE?
2. You can't begin a sentence with a relative clause. TRUE or FALSE?
3. An embedded clause is used at the beginning of a sentence. TRUE or FALSE?

1 False 2 True 3 False

11.6 Parts of speech

Nouns

There are different types of noun:
- **common** – an object you can see or touch, e.g. pen, table, car
- **abstract** – thoughts, ideas, qualities or emotions, e.g. peace, anger, truth
- **collective** – one word indicating a collection of people or objects, e.g. group, herd, queue
- **proper** – an individual name; a place, a person or an object, e.g. Birmingham, Jane, Tower of London.

Noun phrases

A noun phrase is a group of words containing a noun which gives further information about that noun. In the following sentence, the noun phrase is highlighted.

The old, red car parked outside is a nuisance.

A noun phrase can be made up of a number of different elements:
- **head** – this is the noun around which all the other elements are grouped, e.g. **car**
- **determiner** – this comes before the noun and decides what kind of noun is in the phrase: definite, indefinite, common, etc., e.g. **the, some**
- **premodification** – all other words that come before the noun, usually adjectives, e.g. **old, red**
- **postmodification** – all other words in the phrase that come after the noun (head), e.g. **parked outside**.

Pronouns

A **pronoun** takes the place of a **noun** that has already been mentioned: **he, she, it, me, you**. Pronouns can be used as **determiners**. Use of pronouns helps to reduce repetition in your writing, e.g.

John picked up **the ball** and threw **the ball** to **John's** friend.
John picked up **the ball** and threw **it** to **his** friend.

Verbs

A verb makes a noun or pronoun work. There are **three** types of verb.
- **Main** – as a general rule you can put the word '**to**' in front of a main verb: **to walk, to dance, to eat**. These are also known as **full verbs**.
- **Auxiliary** – an auxiliary verb helps the main verb: you **should** walk, he **could** dance, I **might** eat.
- **Primary** – **be**, **have** and **do** can be used as **main** or **auxiliary** verbs:

  They **are** happy. (main)
  They **are** going. (auxiliary)

Finite and non-finite verbs

The finite form of a verb has to change according to number, person or tense.
- **Tense** – I **work** at home. � I **worked** at home.
- **Number** – She **laughs**. ➙ They **laugh**.
- **Person** – I **am** ➙ You **are**

The non-finite form does not show these contrasts. There are **three** non-finite forms:
- **-ed** participle:

  I **dropped** the pencil.
  He was **dropped** from the team.
  They were **dropped** off on the corner.
- **-ing** participle:

  I'm **running** home tonight.
  They're **running** home tonight.
  He was **running** home last night.

- the **base form** of a verb used as an **infinitive**:
  I'll **see**
  They might **see**
  She wants to **see**.

Adjectives

An **adjective** tells us what a noun is like: **old** book, **sensible** child, **smelly** socks. The use of adjectives in your writing will make it more interesting.

Adverbs

An **adverb** tells us how a verb is done: he walked **quickly**, he danced **stylishly**, I ate **greedily**. This kind of adverb is formed by adding **-ly** to an adjective.

Adverbs can also be the **adverbial** element of a **clause**.

An adverbial can be:
- An adverb phrase containing single adverbs
  He ate the cake **greedily**.
- A **prepositional phrase** – a phrase that begins with a preposition
  He ran **to the bus stop**.
- Some sub-ordinate clauses (adverbial clauses)
  I asked him **when he came into the office**.

Adverbials usually answer the question **where**, **when** or **how**.

Many of the descriptions contained in the grammar section are very **brief and general**. For further detail and explanation you should **use a grammar textbook**.

Assessment question answers

Chapter 2

Skellig

You should include the following points in your answers:

1. *blundered*, *walked*, *stumbled*, *climbed*, *shuffled*, *moved*
   They add variety and make the characters seem uncertain.
2. It is a long, complex sentence with lots of clauses; it is repetitive; it creates the effect of a desperate search for Skellig, looking everywhere and getting frustrated.
3. The characters whisper; it's very dark; they are uncertain; there is detail about how they respond to their situation – *our breath was fast, shallow, trembly*; short sentences are used to build up tension; longer sentences create the sense of a search going on.

A Kestrel for a Knave

You should include the following points in your answer:

The description of how dirty Billy is gives the impression he is poor and not well looked after. The way Mr Sugden treats Billy and the way the author emphasises his position of authority – gets other children to act as guards, turns shower to cold, pushes Billy, keeps on punishing even when all the other children realise he's gone too far. The way Billy behaves – unsuccessful attempts to escape, trying to argue with Mr Sugden, giving up and tolerating the spray. The way other children respond to him – laugh and help Mr Sugden but then become uneasy. The author aims to shock the reader with the description of Mr Sugden's bullying behaviour.

Shakespeare

Some guidance about what is required to achieve each level is shown below. It is not specific to any of the plays you may have studied.

To achieve Level 3: A simple retelling of the scenes. Some basic features of language identified but no comment. Some personal response to scenes but no recognition of Shakespeare's purpose. Some recognition of the social or historical context of the play.

To achieve Level 4: A few simple comments about the characters. Answer still focuses on retelling the scenes. Some basic features of language identified with simple comments about Shakespeare's choices. Simple comments show awareness of Shakespeare's purpose in the scenes. Some simple comments on the way the social and historical context of the play informs meaning.

To achieve Level 5: Answer displays a good level of understanding of the characters and their motivation. Comments are supported by reference to the text. Various features of language are identified with explanation and comment showing awareness of the effects of Shakespeare's choices. Shakespeare's purpose and viewpoint clearly identified. Some explanation of the way context informs meaning.

To achieve Level 6: A focused answer with a degree of exploration of the text. Detailed commentary displays understanding of characters, motivation and relationships. Detailed explanation of how language is used and how this contributes to character and atmosphere. References to the text are appropriate and relevant and provide evidence of understanding Shakespeare's viewpoint and purpose, and the effect this has on the reader. Some detailed discussion of the impact of context on meaning.

To achieve Level 7: A full answer showing detailed knowledge of the text and the characters. Sustained focus on the requirements of the question. Detailed and precise analysis of how language contributes to the exploration of characters, motivation, relationships and themes. Some evaluative comments about the way Shakespeare's viewpoint and purpose is established and sustained. Comments show an appreciation of how specific devices and techniques create effects on the reader / audience. Some analysis of the relationship between context and meaning.

Chapter 3

Hide and Seek
1. The boy is playing hide and seek; the boy's friends look for him but then give up and run away; the boy waits for a long time on his own.
2. lonely and nervous
3. Short sentences create tension – he's holding his breath, waiting to be found; question mark shows he's alert to every sound, he seems jumpy and wonders with each noise if they will find him; exclamation marks show fear and excitement.

Nettles
You could comment on the following features of the poem:
- Begins with simple, straightforward language to tell the story.
- Personification of the nettles as soldiers – the *fallen dead*, *recruits*.
- Extended metaphor in the poem of the father's war against the nettles representing his instinctive desire to protect his family from harm.
- Metaphor used in line 3 highlights the poet's hatred of the thing that has hurt his son.
- Language used at the beginning, relating to the young boy, is calm, e.g. *sobs*, *tender*, *soothed* and contrasts with the violent language used later in the poem to relate to the nettles, e.g. *blade*, *slashed*, *fury*, *fierce*.
- The final line extends beyond the meaning of the wounds from the nettles; it refers to the pain the boy will experience as he grows up.

Chapter 4

Newspaper report
1. 27
2. paragraph 4
3. Accept any two of the following: headline, picture, caption, short paragraphs
4. the first sentence
5. *Epic*: makes the journey sound longer, more exciting and dramatic.

National Railway Museum

You could comment on the following features of the leaflet:

Content: balance of information about events and persuasive language; information about new events; emphasis on fun for 'kids'.

Language: use of emotive persuasive language – *incredible, amazing, world record-breaking, futuristic* – comment on the effectiveness of these words; use of words linked to discovery and adventure; use of second person to involve the reader; use of the phrase *it's free* on the front cover.

Layout:

- Pictures – front cover: smiling children appeal to the family, steam train appeals to sense of tradition; inside panel: smiling children, families smiling together, lots of 'hands-on' pictures to show that the exhibitions are interactive.
- Font styles – *it's free* stands out from the background; the rest of the writing on the front cover makes it inviting and appealing, it invites the reader to turn over and open the leaflet up; the text inside the leaflet is in a standard font style and size, it's easy to read and suits the informative purpose of the text.
- Other features – the text is organised by sub-headings; bullet points are used to make the new exhibitions stand out; the whole leaflet is colourful and attractive.
- Effectiveness – include your personal response to the leaflet; decide whether the features you have commented on are used effectively.

Some question-specific guidance is given for what to include in each writing task response on the pages that follow. General APP guidance about what would be required to achieve level 5 and level 7 for each Writing Assessment Focus is shown below.

To achieve level 5:
AF1 – Relevant information and material developed with imaginative detail and shaped to match selected form. Clear viewpoint established.
AF2 – Purpose of writing clear and consistently maintained, features of appropriate form and style are maintained to sustain the reader's interest.
AF3 – Material is structured with sentences organised into paragraphs. Overall direction of text is supported by clear links between paragraphs.
AF4 – Paragraphs clearly structure text to support purpose. Within paragraphs, a range of devices such as connectives support cohesion.
AF5 – Variety of sentence lengths, structures and subjects provide clarity and emphasis. Wide range of connectives used. Some features of sentence structure used to build up detail.
AF6 – Full range of punctuation used accurately to demarcate sentences, including speech punctuation. Syntax and punctuation within sentences generally accurate, including commas to mark clauses.
AF7 – Reasonably wide vocabulary used with choices made for effect.
AF8 – Generally correct spelling including homophones and prefixes and suffixes.

To achieve level 7:

AF1/2 – Imaginative and successful adaptation of range of forms to match purpose and audience. Well judged and distinctive voice and point of view established and sustained. Appropriate level of formality and varied use of stylistic devices.

AF3 – Information, ideas and events managed and shaped to achieve intended purpose and effect.

AF4 – Paragraphing across text is integral to purpose and meaning. Individual paragraphs shaped for imaginative or rhetorical effect.

AF5/6 – Variety of sentence types used with good judgement to achieve desired purpose or effect. Sentences are well controlled. Range of features used to craft individual sentences that add to the overall development of the text.

AF7 – Varied and ambitious range of vocabulary which is consistently and imaginatively matched to purpose and audience.

AF8 – Correct spelling throughout.

Chapter 6

Question 1

Include vocabulary to create a frightening atmosphere. Use a range of complex, compound and simple sentences. Experiment with withholding information to increase tension. Make sure you have a balance of narrative, description and dialogue. Review your vocabulary choices for describing the way characters speak. Give clues about characters, as well as giving explicit description.

Questions 2–4

Make imaginative vocabulary choices to create an atmosphere. Use a range of complex, compound and simple sentences. Experiment with withholding information to increase tension. Experiment with narrative perspective and style. Make sure you have a balance of narrative, description and dialogue. Review your vocabulary choices for describing the way characters speak. Give clues about characters as well as giving explicit description. Develop characterisation and relationships in the middle section of your narrative.

Chapter 7

1. Logical steps or short paragraphs; mostly simple sentences; use imperative; use a range of time connectives; write in the present tense.
2. Introductory paragraph giving an overview of the topic; organise paragraphs by category / topic; use third person; give examples.
3. Use imagery; make imaginative adjective and adverb choices; use a range of complex, compound and simple sentences; describe different aspects of the location – landscape, atmosphere, people, attractions and things to do.
4. Answer each bullet point; use imagery; make imaginative adjective and adverb choices; use a range of complex, compound and simple sentences; describe different aspects of the location – landscape, atmosphere, people, attractions and things to do.
5. Answer each bullet point; use logical, cause and effect connectives; organise into paragraphs.

6. Include information on each of the bullet points; use a range of layout devices; organise information for maximum impact; write in the third person; you could include more personal examples; include facts and statistics.

Chapter 8

1. Write a persuasive introduction; use emotive and persuasive language; use rhetorical questions and statements; use repetition for emphasis; anticipate possible objections and defend against counter-argument.
2. Write a paragraph that introduces the argument and counter-argument; organise paragraphs by argument and counter-argument; give equal weight to each side of the argument; don't give personal opinions except in the conclusion.
3. Answer each bullet point; follow conventions for a formal letter; balance information with persuasive language.
4. Use emotive and persuasive language; use rhetorical questions, statements and exclamations; use repetition for emphasis; anticipate possible objections and defend against counter-argument; use sentence structure to control the pace and emphasis of the speech.
5. Write a paragraph that introduces the argument and counter-argument; organise paragraphs by argument and counter-argument; give equal weight to each side of the argument; don't give personal opinions except in the conclusion.

Chapter 9

Questions 1–2
Include factual information about the piece being reviewed; give your own opinions; consider strengths and weaknesses; justify your opinions with textual evidence, if appropriate; give recommendations.

Questions 3–4
Answer each bullet point; organise paragraphs to build on each point made; use statement – evidence – comment / explanation in each paragraph; follow conventions for including textual evidence; use a formal style; analyse use of particular devices, language or structure where appropriate.

Glossary

Literary terms

Imagery

Image   a picture painted with words. Imagery is used to bring ideas to life and make unusual connections that cause the reader to think.

Metaphor   an assertion that one object is a completely different object – there is no comparison made. *Juliet is the Sun* (from Shakespeare's *Romeo and Juliet*).

- **Extended metaphor**   a metaphor built up from a number of images in a longer piece of text. An extended metaphor can be made up of similes, metaphors and other images.

Oxymoron   the joining of two words or phrases that appear to be complete opposites in meaning: *feather of lead, bright smoke, cold fire, sick health* (from Shakespeare's *Romeo and Juliet*).

Personification   an inanimate (not moving / living) object is given the qualities or actions of a living person or creature: *brightly coloured beach balls dance along the shore*.

Simile   a comparison of two distinctly different objects using the words **like** or **as**: *Her voice cut through him like a knife*.

> **Key Point**   Try to use the correct technical terms when you are writing about literature.

Device

Alliteration   the repetition of a letter or letter sound at the beginning of a sequence of words. Used for emphasis and to link ideas: *the silver snake slithered silently by*.

Assonance   the repetition of identical or similar vowel sounds in a sequence of words: *silent, quiet light, time* (long 'i' sound).

Onomatopoeia   the sound of a word reflects the sound that it describes: *plop, fizz, splash, hiss*.

Structure

Caesura   a pause in the middle of a line of poetry or a sentence in prose, used for dramatic effect.

End-stopped line   in poetry, a full stop or colon at the end of a line causes the reader to pause. This technique is used in combination with enjambment.

Enjambment   this is the technical term for a 'run on line'. When the meaning of one line runs into the next line, there is no punctuation at the end of the line. This technique is used to create a sense of movement or excitement in a poem.

Free verse   describes a poem that has a free structure, without a regular rhyme scheme, rhythm or stanza length.

Rhyme   the ending of one word sounds the same as another: *late / fate, sight / might, health / wealth*

- **End rhymes**   the most common form of rhyme. These rhymes occur at the end of a verse line.

- **Internal rhyme**   these occur in the middle of a verse line: *In mist or cloud, on mast or shroud* (from the *Rime of the Ancient Mariner* by S T Coleridge).

Rhyme scheme   the method of describing rhyme patterns in a poem.

Rhythm   the pattern of beats or stresses in a line or group of lines of poetry, also known as the **meter**.

Stanza   the correct technical term for a verse in poetry.

Other terms

Empathy   writers put themselves in the place of the person or object they are writing about; a stronger sensation than sympathy. If you empathise with somebody, you can understand how they feel and feel their sadness, relief or other emotions yourself.

Narrative   a story told in prose or poetic form. See **Chapter 6** for an explanation of narrative voices.

Narrator   the voice that tells the story.

Key Point   Don't just identify images or devices. You must explain why they are effective.

Glossary of media terms

Newspaper

Broadsheet   a newspaper considered to be more factual and serious than a tabloid. Aims to inform, report and comment, not to entertain. Broadsheets are the larger of the two newspaper styles, e.g. *The Guardian*, *The Times*.

Columns   newspapers and magazine articles are set out in columns; leaflets often use this format too. Columns break up a page and make it more interesting to look at.

Headlines   in newspapers, headlines are particularly important attention grabbers. They are made deliberately dramatic so that the audience will read on. In tabloid newspapers, headlines are often linked to pictures to make up the majority of the front page. Language devices such as alliteration, repetition and rhyme are often used.

Pictures   are used in newspapers to back up, dramatise or personalise a story. They are often closely linked to headlines.

Quotation   a direct comment taken from somebody involved in the news story. This gives the report validity and can often give a more personal feel to the story. Reporters are required to be unbiased, but quotations from other sources will often contain bias.

Short paragraphs   long paragraphs can be off-putting for a busy reader. Most media texts are organised into short paragraphs to hold the reader's attention.

Tabloid   this kind of newspaper is considered to be less serious and sometimes less factual than a broadsheet. Tabloids are also more likely to contain obvious bias. As well as reporting, these newspapers also aim to entertain. They are the smaller of the two newspaper styles, e.g. *The Sun*, *The Mirror*.

Topic sentence   the first sentence in a newspaper story; usually closely linked to the headline. It answers the *who, what, where* and *when* questions.

Advertisements

Personal pronouns   in persuasive writing, particularly advertising and charity campaigns, the pronouns *you* and *we* are used extensively. This is to make the reader feel personally addressed and important.

Pictures   in advertising, the picture can be more important than the text.

Slogans   like a 'catch phrase' linked to the product. Various devices are used to make them more memorable: alliteration, repetition, puns, questions or shocking statements.

Text size   important information is in large print; less appealing information, such as terms and conditions, tends to be in smaller print.

Leaflets

Bold print   darker print makes important information stand out from the rest of the text.

Bullet points   often marked out with an asterisk or small symbol, these short sentences or phrases attract the attention of a busy reader.

Font styles   different styles of printing are used to a make a text look more attractive.

Frames and borders   sections of text may be presented within a border or box to make them stand out or to separate them from other information.

Graphs and charts   are used to demonstrate facts and figures in a clear visual way.

Pictures   are often used in an emotive way in leaflets, e.g. a picture of a starving African child or a lonely pensioner.

Sub-headings   are used as signposts to indicate important information in any text. Key words and phrases are picked out to focus the reader's attention.

Other terms

Audience   a term to describe the readership that a particular text is aimed at. In advertising, a lot of market research is done so that products can be aimed at very specific groups of people – the people most likely to buy the product.

Market research   is used by advertising companies to find out the preferences of an identified group of people. The information collected will influence decisions about colours, music, language, age and styling of actors used in advertising campaigns, as well as the pricing and packaging of products.

Tone of voice   this indicates the emotions and feelings that the writer wishes to convey. It is easy to identify a tone of voice when somebody is speaking to you; it is more difficult to identify the tone of a piece of writing. You can identify tone of voice by examining the vocabulary choices, formality, structure and content of a piece of writing. Tones of voice you might expect to find in media texts are: persuasive, conversational, informative, tempting, dramatic or conspiratorial. You wouldn't expect the tone to be aggressive or superior, as this would be off-putting.

Assessment focuses

APP and **Optional Tests** are used to determine your **National Curriculum level** in each **Assessment Focus**.

In **Speaking and Listening**, the Assessment Focuses are:
AF1 Talking to others – Talk in purposeful and imaginative ways to explore ideas and feelings, adapting and varying structure and vocabulary according to purpose, listeners, and content.
AF2 Talking with others – Listen and respond to others, including in pairs and groups, shaping meanings through suggestions, comments and questions.
AF3 Talking within role-play and drama – Create and sustain different roles and scenarios, adapting techniques in a range of dramatic activities to explore texts, ideas and issues.
AF4 Talking about talk – Understand the range and uses of spoken language, commenting on meaning and impact, and draw on this when talking to others.

In **Reading**, the Assessment Focuses are:
AF1 – Use a range of strategies, including accurate decoding of text, to read for meaning. (This AF is not tested directly in Optional Tests. It assesses whether you can understand what you have read. In the APP grid there is only a description for levels 2 and 3.)
AF2 – Understand, describe, select or retrieve information, events or ideas from texts and use quotation and reference to text.
AF3 – Deduce, infer or interpret information, events or ideas from texts.
AF4 – Identify and comment on the structure and organisation of texts, including grammatical and presentational features at text level.
AF5 – Explain and comment on writers' use of language, including grammatical and literary features at word and sentence level.
AF6 – Identify and comment on writers' purposes and viewpoints, and the overall effect of the text on the reader.
AF7 – Relate texts to their social, cultural and historical traditions.

In **Writing**, the Assessment Focuses are:
AF1 – Write imaginative and thoughtful texts.
AF2 – Produce texts which are appropriate to task, reader and purpose.
AF3 – Organise and present whole texts effectively, sequencing and structuring information, ideas and events.
AF4 – Construct paragraphs and use cohesion within and between paragraphs.
AF5 – Vary sentences for clarity, purpose and effect.
AF6 – Write with technical accuracy of syntax and punctuation in phrases, clauses and sentences.
AF7 – Select appropriate and effective vocabulary.
AF8 – Use correct spelling.

The AFs for Speaking and Listening are covered in Chapter 1. The AFs for Reading are covered in Chapters 2–4. The AFs for Writing are covered in Chapters 5–11.

Acknowledgements

The authors and publisher are grateful to the copyright holders for permission to use quoted materials:

pp17, 18, 19: 'Harry Potter and the Philosopher's Stone' - Copyright © J K Rowling 1997. Reprinted by permission of the author and Christopher Little Literary Agency.

p20: Extract from **Kit's Wilderness** by David Almond, first published by Hodder Children's Books, and reproduced by permission of the author c/o The Maggie Noach Literary Agency. Copyright © David Almond 1999.

pp22–23: From A KESTREL FOR A KNAVE by Barry Hines (Michael Joseph, 1968) Copyright © Barry Hines, 1968.

pp25–26: Robert Swindells, Room 13 (Heinemann New Windmill, 1998). Reprinted by permission of The Random House Group Ltd.

p36: Extract from **Skellig** by David Almond, first published by Hodder Children's Books, and reproduced by permission of the author c/o The Maggie Noach Literary Agency. Copyright © David Almond 1999.

p39: Charles Causley, "What has happened to Lulu?" from "Collected Poems" (Picador, London). Reprinted by permission of David Higham Associates Ltd.

p41: "City Jungle" by Pie Corbett. © Pie Corbett. From Rice, Pie and Moses by John Rice, Pie Corbett and Brian Moses, published by Macmillan, London, 1995.

p.42: Excerpt from 'Valentine' is taken from "Mean Time" by Carol Ann Duffy published by Anvil Press Poetry in 1993. Reprinted by permission.

p44: 'Cold Knap Lake' from 'Collected Poems' by Gillian Clarke (Carcanet, 1997). Reprinted by permission of Carcanet Press Limited.

p54:"Hide and Seek" by Vernon Scannell © Vernon Scannell. Reprinted by permission of the Literary Executor for the Estate of Vernon Scannell.

p.55 "Nettles" from "New and Collected Poems" by Vernon Scannell © Vernon Scannell. Reprinted by permission of the Literary Executor for Estate of Vernon Scannell.

p57: From Cider with Rosie by Laurie Lee, published by Chatto & Windus. Reprinted by permission of The Random House Group Ltd.

pp61, 62–63: From Notes from a Small Island by Bill Bryson, published by Doubleday. Reprinted by permission of The Random House Group Ltd.

pp63–64: "The Upright Ape", reprinted by permission of The Yorkshire Museum, York.

p74: National Railway Museum (York) leaflet (2001), reprinted with permission.

p84: From A KESTREL FOR A KNAVE by Barry Hines (Michael Joseph, 1968) Copyright © Barry Hines, 1968.

p85: From OF MICE AND MEN by John Steinbeck (Penguin, 2000) © Copyright John Steinbeck, 1937, 1965;

p85: Iain M Banks Excession © Iain M Banks (1996) Orbit books, an imprint of Little, Brown Book Group as publisher. Reproduced by permission.

pp86–87: H G Wells, "The Red Room" from Stories Then and Now (Heinemann New Windmill 1997) with permission of A P Watt Ltd on behalf of the Literary Executors of the Estate of H G Wells.

pp89, 90–91: Extracts from **Kit's Wilderness** by David Almond, first published by Hodder Children's Books, and reproduced by permission of the author c/o The Maggie Noach Literary Agency. Copyright © David Almond 1999.

p93: From STONE COLD by Robert Swindells (Hamish Hamilton, 1993) Copyright © Robert Swindells, 1993.

p111: Friends of the Earth campaign letter (edited version), reprinted by kind permission of Friends of the Earth.

Every effort has been made to trace the copyright holders and to obtain their permission for the use of copyright material. The author and publisher will gladly receive information enabling them to rectify any error or omission in subsequent editions.

Index